THE TRUE
PATHS TO
MEDITATION

From shodo—"the Way of calligraphy"—to budo—"the martial Way"—the Japanese have succeeded in designing their traditional arts and crafts as paths to meditation. The names of these skills frequently end with the word Do, also pronounced Michi, which equals the "Way." When practicing a Way, we unearth universal principles that go beyond a specific discipline, relating to the art of living itself. Featuring the books of H. E. Davey and other select writers, works by Michi Publishing center on these Do forms. Michi Publishing's focus is on classical Asian arts, spirituality, and meditation, benefiting all cultures.

THE TRUE PATHS TO MEDITATION

Sawai Atsuhiro

Michi Publishing
Albany, California

NOTE TO READERS

Shin-shin-toitsu-do, a.k.a. Japanese yoga/meditation, involves the movement of both mind and body. As with any form of physical exercise or psychological practice, if the techniques depicted in this book are misused, misinterpreted, or wrongly practiced, injuries and other problems may result. The author and publisher will not be held responsible in any manner for any injuries or damage of any kind that may occur as the result of following the directions offered in this book. No claims regarding the suitability of any of the methods described or illustrated in this book for the treatment of any physical or psychological disorder are made or should be inferred. Readers are urged to seek appropriate medical and psychological advice before undertaking the practice of Japanese yoga/meditation or any of the procedures presented in this book. Readers are also advised to perform the methods outlined in this book only under the direct supervision of a trained teacher.

The True Paths to Meditation by Sawai Atsuhiro
Text and photographs © 2013 Michi Publishing
All rights reserved. No part of this book may be reproduced in any form without written permission from the publisher.

ISBN (softcover): 978-0-9904214-0-5
ISBN (ebook): 978-0-9904214-1-2

Published by Michi Publishing
Albany, California
www.michipublishing.com

10 9 8 7 6 5 4 3 2 1

Photography by Ann Kameoka
Book design by Sun Editing & Book Design, suneditwrite.com
Cover photo of the author by Masuda Kozo

Printed and bound in the United States of America

CONTENTS

AN INTRODUCTION TO MEDITATION

I have been practicing meditation for over 50 years since I began to study it under the guidance of Nakamura Tempu Sensei, the founder of *Shin-shin-toitsu-do*, a famous form of Japanese yoga emphasizing mind and body unification. I also studied Zen meditation with my uncle Yamazaki Shuzan. He learned Zen in his childhood, and he practiced at the famous Tenryu Temple. Later, he became head priest at Shoden Temple in Kyoto. He also took me to lectures on Zen Buddhism by other celebrated priests in Nara and Kyoto.

Over the last 50 years or so, I've come to realize that there are numerous mistaken concepts and methods concerning meditation among many people in the world. My experiences prompted me to write a book on meditation, so that I might offer a new explanation of meditation practice to the world.

Emptying the Mind

A few years ago, I wrote *Kokoro o Ku ni Suru: Nakamura Tempu's Shin-shin-toitsu-ho* ("Emptying the Mind: Nakamura Tempu's Methods of Unifying Mind and Body") in Japanese. It was published in February 2009, and this let me discuss meditation with many readers in Japan. They asked me unexpected questions and left me thinking from several different angles about how to write about meditation. Since the publication of the book, not a single day has passed without me pondering how to describe meditation so people can improve their understanding of it.

My primary teacher of yoga, Nakamura Sensei, was a great practitioner of meditation, and so was one of his students, Oki Masahiro Sensei, who also established his own school of Japanese yoga. (*Sensei* is an honorific title meaning "teacher.") I studied meditation with both of them, and I found that because they had achieved such an unusually high level of mental development, they couldn't easily express how to meditate to ordinary readers. They were talented advocators of meditation, but better practitioners than writers. These factors motivated me to act as a "bridge" between their teachings of meditation and the general public, and I decided to write books on meditation practice to facilitate this.

My book *Emptying the Mind* reached the top of the bestseller list in Japan for two months, and the first edition sold out in two weeks. As numerous Japanese friends of mine living abroad, mainly in the United States, came to know of my book, they suggested that I translate it into English. I thought about their suggestion, but I wrote that book exclusively for Japanese readers, which makes the book difficult for an English-speaking audience to relate to.

Meditation: It's Not As Difficult As You Think

This prompted me to write a wholly new book on meditation for Western audiences, which I've titled *The True Paths to Meditation*. In this book, I cover some misunderstandings about meditation that I have found to be common:

- People wrongly believe that they have to sit still for long hours to practice meditation.

- They wrongly believe they must sit in strange, difficult, and painful postures.

- They do not realize they can easily arrive at meditation by following proper methods of concentration as a prelude to meditation.

* They do not know they can enjoy marvelous benefits from meditation by meditating alone every day.

Concerning the time we spend on meditation, it is useless to sit for long hours if we have not grasped the true feeling of meditation. I also seriously doubt that we need to sit in large groups of practitioners to arrive at meditation.

I studied meditation directly under Nakamura Sensei for twelve years, until he passed away in 1968, and what I understood from him was that real meditation lies in the depths of calmness, not in the length of time we sit. I also learned two methods of concentration that lead us to meditation, which I will write about in upcoming chapters.

Not only can you not meditate, however long you sit, if you have not grasped what meditation is, but sitting for hours never fails to cause unbearable pain in your legs. This rarely leads to good meditation. Real meditation never gives you any pains or extreme discomfort, though when you are a beginner, you may have to endure some minor soreness. If you feel any torment after you learn it, you are not in the true state of meditation.

The Benefits of Meditation

If you meditate just twenty minutes every day, you can feel the true meaning and excellent effects of meditation. The effects/purposes of meditation are varied, and I will later write about them. However, here is a brief summary of some benefits of meditation:

1. Meditation promotes mental health, because it makes your mind clear and calm, which will eventually help you physically, too.

2. Meditation encourages positive thinking, heightens mental capabilities, and develops concentration. This helps you make good decisions, especially during important moments in your life.

3. Meditation helps you find your true self, which leads to *satori*, or spiritual enlightenment.

The first and second benefits appeal to more pragmatic individuals, while the third may appeal to more spiritually oriented people. I believe both utilitarian and spiritual approaches to meditation are fine, and even though the third is the most admirable road to meditation, those who enter meditation by the first and second

11

gates will someday want to pass through the third gate. I wanted to study meditation mainly to improve my health. But soon I found the real goal of meditation is to know your true self. Many people began to study it for reasons similar to mine.

Positions for Seated Meditation

I will explain shortly more about correct posture during meditation and some sitting positions. However, what is more important is to know the right feeling when you enter meditation. Then you can improve the position you sit in gradually after that. Although both Zen and yoga advocate the "lotus posture," if you are a beginner and stick to this classical way of sitting, you will find it difficult to focus your attention. This sitting arrangement is initially uncomfortable and distracting for most people, and therefore they cannot reach the state of meditation.

Please remember you must know how to develop deep concentration before you can fall into meditation. Too much thought about the position you sit in tends to prevent you from concentrating. You can sit in a chair, not on the floor, if you prefer it. Especially those who have something wrong with their legs or knees are advised to use a comfortable chair.

Those who have reached a higher level in meditation can study more traditional positions, in order to advance in their practice. I believe meditation should be and can be learned in a freer atmosphere than is sometimes present in certain approaches, and I believe ordinary students can enjoy it. Real meditation makes people comfortable and happy. If well guided, many people can enjoy meditation practice every day.

Concentration Leads to Meditation

You have to study how to concentrate preceding meditation and how this concentrated condition allows you to fall into the state of meditation. Meditation is a state of mind that is, "doing nothing, thinking nothing" to quote H. E. Davey Sensei, the American author of *Japanese Yoga: The Way of Dynamic Meditation* and a teacher of Nakamura Sensei's methods.

If you have learned how to concentrate, you can naturally enter the domain of meditation—that is doing nothing, thinking nothing. Meditation relates to *muga munen*, terminology originating in Zen. Here, munen means literally "no thoughts," but it can more easily be understood as "no distractions." Munen is a state of mind without mental wandering—a pure and lucid mind like the surface of a polished mirror that reflects objects clearly and precisely. Munen is also a positive and strong mind, a mind free from conflicts. It is a mind as reflective as a calm lake in a deep mountain forest, which reflects the surrounding scenery as clearly as a mirror. In a word, muga munen is the realization of our real self, a self that is free from any conflicts. In this state, we move beyond our attachments to thought and realize calmness in meditation.

But what about muga? Muga means literally "no self," but this literal translation can be misleading, and in upcoming chapters I'll more clearly explain muga. Unfortunately, how to concentrate and produce muga have been problems for innumerable people.

There have been countless suggested methods of concentration since ancient times, but most of them have not been easily accomplished. Remember first that a method of concentration must be simple and concrete. The complicated imagining of a lotus flower for example, as some teachers advocate, is neither.

Muga is to grasp one's real self by initially concentrating on one point. It can be done in several ways. When you listen to your favorite music or when you are deeply engaged in one of your hobbies, you are usually in muga. But it is doubtful whether you will be able to be in meditation after you have experienced the state of muga. This is because meditation is, as I mentioned above, both muga and munen at the same time. When munen is realized, along with muga, there is no mental wandering.

Even after you attempt to throw away distractions and are absorbed in something, some thoughts will often remain in your mind. For example, after you have listened to music, the emotions that the music caused in you will possibly remain in your consciousness. It is for this reason that something like music is not suitable for concentration practice that leads to meditation. So, an object we use for concentration-meditation must be simpler and not raise any thoughts or emotions.

What object is good for concentration has been pondered for thousands of years, since yoga was born in India. There is a long human history of struggling to find really effective methods to realize meditation. Numerous methods of concentration used in meditation, however, were too complicated or too abstract to be effective. An example is a practice in which students try to become one with their sitting posture, but to be one with a posture is an idea too vague and too abstract. Thus concentration cannot be gained easily in that way. Some people recommend imagining a religious symbol or idol, but it is harder to realize meditation (muga munen) in that way, as imagined objects can evoke thoughts or sensations negating true meditation.

Meditation is a mental state that is completely calm and clear of any specific thought or visualized image.

Nakamura Sensei, and some Indian yoga teachers that predate him, discovered simple and effective methods for concentration. Their methods are revolutionary and easy to practice, so easy that numerous people fail to see their true value. I will introduce them later in detail, and I hope you will enjoy both *The True Paths to Meditation* and meditation itself.

The Contents of the Book

All of the above is to quickly give you a sense of who I am and what I'll be writing about in this book. It is a general orientation and not meant to be a complete explanation of meditation. That's what the subsequent chapters are for.

Chapters One and Two show you concrete methods of concentration that then lead to meditation. In Chapter Three, I'll discuss what meditation is, quoting some explanations of it by yoga authorities and researchers. Chapter Four presents the major benefits and purposes of meditation, and it shows how meditation is useful and valuable in daily life. In Chapter Five, I will write about my personal experiences with yogic meditation. And in Chapter Six I discuss the problems facing humanity in the 21st century, and I explain how meditation can resolve them.

In the book's appendices, I cover the relationship between philosophy, religion, and science, while I show how yogic meditation can unite these fields of human activity. Also explained are the differences and similarities between yoga and Zen Buddhism as well as how they have been related to each other in the long cultural history of India, China, and Japan. I also present a brief survey of recent advanced scientific research into how meditation affects brain waves and how beneficial meditation is for mental and physical health. The book concludes with information about obtaining further instruction, meditation bells, and meditation CDs, along with a useful glossary of terms related to the topics that have been discussed.

Acknowledgements

The True Paths to Meditation would not exist if it were not for the help of several important people in my life. As this book begins, I'd like to acknowledge them.

I owe much to my superb teachers of meditation: Nakamura Tempu Sensei, Oki Masahiro Sensei, Tamaki Koshiro Sensei, and Sahota Tsuruji Sensei. I will write about them in forthcoming chapters.

I am grateful to H. E. Davey Sensei for his efforts to correct and improve my English and for his editing of this book. I appreciate his encouragement and fine advice. He is my good friend and an established professional writer in the United States. I also admire his continuous study and practice of Nakamura Sensei's teachings for many years and his devoted efforts to teach Japanese yoga/meditation to Americans. He has an excellent dojo (training hall) called the Sennin Foundation Center for Japanese Cultural Arts near the University of California in Berkeley, where he teaches not only Nakamura Sensei's meditation, but also Japanese martial arts, healing arts, and brush calligraphy.

I appreciate Troy Swenson Sensei posing for the photos in this book. Mr. Swenson is a teacher of Japanese yoga and meditation at the Sennin Foundation Center. He also received *Koshi* teaching certification from our International Japanese Yoga Association in Kyoto. I am also grateful to Ann Kameoka Sensei, another student of Japanese yoga, who took the photos used in my book.

I would like to thank Hiroko Dewitz for encouraging me to publish an English language book on meditation. She is head of the Honolulu Foundation, a nonprofit organization, which provides the general public with opportunities to study the ideas of Nakamura Sensei and other eminent Japanese philosophers and thinkers.

I also would like to thank Hashimoto Koji for his encouragement, advice, and support. He is a great practitioner of Nakamura Sensei's Shin-shin-toitsu-do and the manager of a group that studies Nakamura Sensei's methods in Kobe, Japan.

I am grateful to Michi Publishing for their efforts in producing this work. More than this, I am grateful for their friendship and support.

It is due to my involvement in the yogic meditation of Nakamura Sensei that I met Sawai Yoko, my wife, who has been a constant source of help in every aspect of my life.

Lastly, I'd like to thank you for buying this book. I hope meditation will help you as much as it's helped me.

Sawai Atsuhiro
Kyoto, Japan

Chapter 1

MUGA ICHI-NEN HO: THE TRANSITION FROM CONCENTRATION TO MEDITATION

In this book's Introduction to Meditation I mentioned that however many hours you sit with closed eyes, you cannot reach true meditation, if you do not know a good method to arrive at concentration. Most people trying to meditate find that various thoughts or sensations come up one after another in the mind; it is far from the clear, calm consciousness they seek in meditation.

What you must do (at first) to arrive at meditation is concentrate properly on one point, and this will allow you to grasp the real state of meditation. Despite what some believe, this is the real key to meditating, not enduring the pain of sitting hours in some arduous position. Being mistaken about this point can result in you wasting a great deal of time.

The 21st century is seeing an explosive influx of varied information due to the advent of the Internet and other forms of mass communication. Even once secret methods of yogic meditation have become known in recent years. Some Indian yoga adepts and Nakamura Tempu Sensei, a Japanese yoga teacher, have made effective meditation methods known to the general public, but lots of us are still badly informed about the real value of meditation and what constitutes efficient methods of concentration that can lead to genuine meditation. This is partly because so much information concerning yoga and meditation has flooded the Internet and our local bookstores, with many of the teachings contradicting each other. We don't know where to begin and which methods to trust.

It's little wonder that some individuals believe ordinary people cannot easily reach the state of meditation, thinking that only great saints, sages, or religious leaders can achieve meditative consciousness, and even then only after enduring hard practice for countless years. However, by practicing the methods of concentration I am going to introduce, anyone can experience real meditation. No special talent or long years of training are needed, but you must be earnest and serious.

These methods do not take much time to read about or practice. And even if you just experience a few minutes of meditation, it will be of great significance in your future life.

Muga Ichi-nen

"Concentration and meditation are united like a stream, forming one method of mental training."

—Sahoda Tsuruji
Yoga Konpon Kyoten[1]

Sahoda Tsuruji Sensei is an esteemed scholar and practitioner of yoga, who translated the famed *Yoga Sutras* into Japanese from their original Sanskrit. He studied philosophy at Kyoto University and taught philosophy as a professor at Ritsumeikan University and Osaka University. Despite his excellent works like *Yoga Konpon Kyoten*, numerous Japanese are still confused about the relationship between concentration and meditation, and I think the same is true for inhabitants of the Western nations I've visited.

Some people think concentration training and meditation are two different kinds of practice. In reality, concentration and meditation are connected like different sections of the same river. Concentration flows into meditation.

But what is concentration and how can we get the feeling of truly concentrating? The answer is straightforward: to concentrate you just have to center your attention on one thought (*ichi-nen*). Focusing the mind on one point or one object of concentration can do this.

How do we know when we've done it successfully? If the mind attends completely to a single point of concentration, so that this thought fills the entire consciousness, then this puts the mind in the state of muga. Muga means literally "no self," "no self-consciousness," or "forgetting about yourself" by concentrating on one thing. In Nakamura Sensei's Shin-shin-toitsu-do Japanese yoga, we call this condition in which the mind is focused in the present, by concentrating on a single thought, muga ichi-nen— "no self, one thought." Nakamura Sensei's form of meditation based on this idea is *Muga Ichi-nen Ho*, the "Muga Ichi-nen Method."

Concentrating on one thought, until we no longer worry about ourselves, leads to the calmness we typically associate with meditation. When you reach the stage of meditation, your mind will become both muga and munen. Munen literally means "no thought, no sensation," but it truly means doing nothing, think-ing nothing. In this condition, we are wholly in the moment, without worrying about the past, the future, or ourselves.

Muga Munen

If you think, on the other hand, that when you transcend the individual self by concentrating on one thought, you've realized meditation, you are mistaken. True meditation is the state of muga *plus* munen. It is to bring the mind totally into the moment, a moment both endless and eternal, through concentrating on some object existing in the present. At this instant, the mind is completely alert, merging with the object of concentration to transcend itself. This is muga ichi-nen.

But the mind is still bound to the object of concen-tration, which we must also transcend. When this is accomplished, the mind is entirely alert; resting calmly in the present, but it is clear and "empty." This allows the mind to accurately reflect whatever is taking place at the moment. In other words, we use an object of concentration to awaken the mind and lead us beyond distracting thoughts, by focusing on a single thought. But eventually, to arrive at meditation, we must learn to let this final thought go. This is muga munen.

In short, muga ichi-nen—"going beyond self-consciousness while focused on one thought"—is concentration. Muga munen—"going beyond self-consciousness while transcending all attachments to thought"—is meditation.

Objects of Concentration

In Asia, countless methods of concentration have been presented and taught by numerous teachers. The objects that have been recommended for concentration and/or meditation are also many. The following are some common examples:

- The navel
- The tip of the nose
- A lotus flower in the region of the heart
- A light within the head

These are but a few places where meditators sometimes attempt to center their minds. While it is possible to concentrate on anything, some methods are easier than others.

The navel and the tip of the nose, for instance, cannot be seen during sitting meditation, making them harder to concentrate on. We often find that we pay attention to what we can see; using visible objects can make concentration easier. And a lotus inside the heart and a light within the head must be imagined, sometimes rendering whatever we conjure up vague and difficult to pay attention to.

We can realize muga ichi-nen (concentration) to some extent by imagining such objects, but it is hard to reach muga munen (meditation), as all of these points of focus require imagination, which often drifts in and out of focus. Plus, these imagined formations could leave some thought and/or sensation in our minds.

In a few paragraphs, I'll explain Nakamura Sensei's easier method to arrive at muga ichi-nen, one that will eventually allow you to transcend attachments to thought and arrive at muga munen—the state of genuine meditation.

Real Concentration Leads to Real Meditation

"Obstacles to meditation can be eliminated
by concentrating on one object."

—Patanjali
The Yoga Sutras[2]

Yoga and its related methods of meditation have achieved worldwide acclaim in recent years, with even physicians and psychologists in numerous countries recommending the practice of yoga and/or meditation for the reduction of anxiety attacks, lowering blood pressure, and dealing with various forms of stress. Many yoga teachers have their own (often widely differing) points of view about innumerable issues relating to meditation, but they frequently are of one mind as to the importance of one-pointedness in practicing concentration-meditation.

In this sense, they are echoing the advice of perhaps the most famous authority on yoga, Patanjali, who edited *The Yoga Sutras* in ancient India. Gradually, Patanjali's ideas spread beyond India to Japan, Europe, and the USA, where contemporary yoga authorities also avow the importance of concentration, although not always in the clearest manner.

My friend H. E. Davey Sensei, the American author of several books relating to meditation, regularly advises his students that "concentration is a preamble to meditation." Elise Everarda, a Dutch researcher and practitioner of yoga, says, "The Yogis know of many ways to bring the mind to a state of concentration or one-pointed focus."[3] And in 1958, Mircea Eliade, a French authority on yoga, indicated in *Yoga: Immortality and Freedom* that concentration is, in fact, fixing the attention on one point. Eliade went on to state that the yogi sits still, breathing rhythmically, eyes and concentration on an individual point, and in doing so, he or she experiences a passing beyond the materialistic realm of life. He begins to become self-governing in relationship to the universe; external stress no longer bothers him.

Eliade also wrote that the *yogin* (*yogi*, or yoga practitioner) becomes insensible to heat and cold, light and darkness, and other forms of sensory input. Unfortunately, I think this point is commonly misunderstood, and before we can begin concentration-based meditation, I want to address it.

Real concentration is not a trance-like condition. Such a condition, in which the senses shut down and no longer report external sensations, cannot easily be integrated into life. We cannot drive, for example, while insensitive to light and dark, heat and cold. Yet what we learn via real concentration and meditation *can* be related to daily living if properly understood and explained.

The yogi clearly senses hot and cold, but they do not distract him. He perceives various sensations, but he has learned to not be attached to what he perceives. His mental stream is concentrated and unified.

To misunderstand this is to hopelessly try to shut out everything our senses report from the outside world in an attempt to arrive at meditation in an exclusively inner world. This only leaves us vulnerable to the outside world, while our inner realm struggles to block out that which is external. This results in constant tension, and even if we succeed in shutting down our senses, we then leave ourselves helpless and unable to deal with a fire in our home or an intruder. Yet real meditation should make us safer and stronger, both mentally and physically. It doesn't involve superhuman feats or rendering ourselves insensible to all stimuli. It is simply the act of concentration without clinging to whatever our senses report.

Muga Ichi-nen Ho Meditation

Now, I would like to introduce a concrete method of concentration that leads to meditation, which I learned from Nakamura Sensei. When you read the following explanation, you will see how simple meditation can be; if you seriously practice what follows, you'll discover how profoundly meditation can affect your life.

Step One: Muga Ichi-nen

Sit with an erect, but comfortable posture, either on the floor or on a firm chair. Draw a small black dot on a piece of white paper as in **Figure 1**. Watch it closely and intently to arrive at powerful concentration, which leads to effective meditation.

I advise beginners to draw a larger dot at first, and then make a smaller one in accordance with your progress. As concentration advances, it is possible to focus efficiently on a smaller point.

Step Two: Muga Munen

Watch this black circle for a few seconds, close your eyes, and then you will see a reversed light colored dot showing up on your retinas. Continue gazing at the reversed image of the dot until it has gradually and completely disappeared.

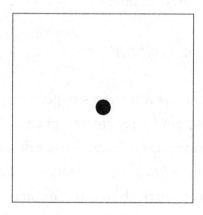

FIGURE 1: *Focus on a dot and forget your self. Then, close your eyes and watch the fading afterimage. Finally, watch nothingness itself in a state beyond your impermanent self and thoughts.*

When the reversed image fades from your retinas entirely, you can feel muga munen, or thinking nothing, doing nothing. But this may only last for two or three seconds. After a few minutes, if you feel unsettled or find yourself daydreaming, simply open your eyes, look at the dot, and start the process again.

Don't worry about how long you can sustain muga munen. You just have to grasp the deep calmness that arises at the point of transition from "no self, one thought" to "no self, no thoughts." This profound composure is the true state of a mind in meditation, and you'll progressively learn to remain in this state for longer periods. Once you have grasped the feeling of deep tranquility, you can lead your mind back to this profound calmness at any time.

Advice for Beginners

It may take many attempts to get a real feeling for muga munen, but be patient and practice Muga Ichi-nen Ho again and again. In time, you will reach intense concentration followed by meditation. The focus and tranquility you reach during the meditation practice will heighten your ability to concentrate. A mind that can sustain concentration when considering an issue in life can often also hit upon new, creative ideas and solutions to problems. A daily Muga Ichi-nen Ho practice requires willpower, so it also strengthens your will, allowing you to more easily control your mind and body.

Meditation cannot be fully explained in a book, and to genuinely grasp it, you'll need to watch the black dot, and then gaze at the afterimage on your retinas, again and again. When you are fully centered on this image, your mind is in the state of muga ichi-nen, and you have good concentration. If you do this practice just 20 minutes or so every day at your home or office when you have a few spare minutes, you will soon come to know what true meditation is.

My teacher Nakamura Sensei introduced this meditation in one of his books, *Anjo Daza Kosho* ("A Booklet on Anjo Daza Meditation"), where he proposed watching any one object before you. His student Yamada Chikaaki Sensei, one of my friends, earnestly followed and advocated this meditative method of watching one object. Mr. Yamada practiced Muga Ichi-nen Ho very seriously and credited his practice with helping him to detect the existence of numerous iron mines, when he was a mine engineer. He was a graduate of Tokyo University's Technology Department, eventually becoming CEO of a company. Even as a senior citizen, he remained mentally sharp and exhibited good judgment until he died at the age of 94 in 2006. He attributed his professional success and fine mental state to daily Muga Ichi-nen Ho, and the benefits he received from its practice are common among Nakamura Sensei's students in Japan.

If you keep doing this simple method, you can eventually experience satori, the spiritual realization that many towering figures in history have alluded to, as meditation is thought to be basic and necessary in countless philosophies and forms of spirituality. Buddha is said to have reached satori, or enlightenment, by practicing meditation, which allowed him to establish Buddhism. But profound spiritual experiences are not limited to Buddha or to those that follow Buddhism. Regardless of our beliefs, or who we are, we can also experience spiritual awakening through meditation.

You need not depend on any instructor or school to perform this kind of meditation. You only need to make a strong decision to practice the above-mentioned method of watching one point. Each of us can (and must) discover meditation firsthand and through our own efforts.

With sincere effort, this method will ensure your good mental health due to deeper levels of calmness, relaxation, concentration and willpower, byproducts of real meditation. Since the mind controls the body, with calmness influencing blood pressure, heart rate, respiration, blood circulation, and the immune system, in no time Muga Ichi-nen Ho will positively impact your physical health, too. Additionally, because meditation leads to serenity—something much more comfortable than nervousness—we feel more at ease in life, which makes it easier to realize positive thinking. If you feel more at ease in your own skin, you'll find that a positive attitude is more readily sustained, and most of us know that such an attitude is advantageous in life.

Correct Posture

Nakamura Sensei encouraged his students to meditate with an erect posture. He also told us that this should be a posture that we could easily maintain, over an extended period of time, as we sit motionless. This means the posture of meditation should be expansive, but not overly erect and rigid. It is not limp and slumped over, nor is it tense and stiff.

While correct posture is important in meditation, the exact position you sit in is not. Select a position that is comfortable for you. There are several that students of Shin-shin-toitsu-do ("The Way of Mind and Body Unification") commonly use. One is the lotus position that is utilized in both Zen and yoga. You can see an example of the "full lotus position" in **Figure 2**. An easier way of sitting is the "half lotus position" seen in **Figure 3**. It is also possible to sit Japanese-style, lightly on your heels, as in **Figure 4**. These positions all encourage good posture, but they can be hard on your legs until you get used to them.

You need not suffer to sit in meditation. Simply sit on a firm chair, with an erect (but not tense) posture, like in **Figure 5**. If you are not feeling well, you can even meditate while lying on your back.

FIGURE 2: *This is the lotus position. Sit lightly on the floor, with a big and erect posture. Keep the lower back straight, the chest open, and the shoulders down. The right foot is on the left thigh, the left foot is on the right thigh, and the left leg is on top. The eyes are gently closed.*

FIGURE 3: *This is the half lotus position. Sit lightly on the floor, with a big and erect posture. Keep the lower back straight, the chest open, and the shoulders down. The right foot is tucked in, close to the groin, and the left foot rests on top of the right thigh. The eyes are gently closed.*

FIGURE 4: *This position is called seiza. Sit lightly on your heels, with some space between your knees, and the big toes crossed. Maintain an expansive, erect posture. Keep the lower back straight, the chest open, and the shoulders down. The eyes are gently closed.*

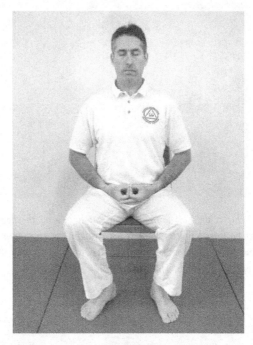

FIGURE 5: *Pick a firm chair for meditation. Sit lightly on the seat, with both feet close to the chair. Maintain an expansive, erect posture. Keep the lower back straight, the chest open, and the shoulders down. The eyes are gently closed.*

Alternative Methods

You can use alternate figures as in **Figure 6** for a change of mood, but more complicated ones are not recommended because they tend to evoke needless thoughts, causing the mind to wander. Simple patterns are better for concentration.

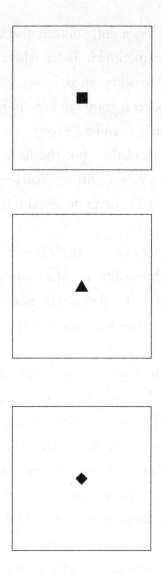

FIGURE 6: *Use these shapes as an alternative to the dot. Concentrate on any of them to realize "no self, one thought." Then, softly close your eyes and watch the diminishing afterimage. When you can't see it, do nothing and let the feeling of calmness continue.*

Instead of using a dot, you can also watch a candle flame, a common method in India, where this variant of Muga Ichi-nen Ho is known as *Trataka*. To acquire this skill, there are several points to keep in mind.

First, watching a candle for long periods can irritate your eyes. To avoid this, put the flame a few meters away from where you are sitting. You only need to look at the candle until your mind is centered on its light; don't overdo it.

Second, do not put the candle near a draft. You have to use candlelight meditation in a room with no breeze flowing in. Then the flame will not flicker, staying unwavering for a few seconds at least. This makes it easier to concentrate on.

Third, try to imprint the image of the light on your retinas. When you later close your eyes, it will be reversed and become a bluish black dot on them. It is crucial that you look intently at it until it fades. Then you can concentrate the mind in the present moment and forget about yourself, which is meditation. Watching the fading reversed image of the candle flame, as far as I know, is less commonly espoused, which is why I've added some additional explanation.

Finally, sometimes the reversed afterimage seems to have disappeared but appears again later. Sometimes the dot moves its position slightly on the retinas. Don't

worry about any of this; just keep focusing your attention on it. When you find it completely gone from the
retinas, watch the "nothingness," and you will fall into
muga munen, thinking nothing and doing nothing. You
will not become senseless or lose your consciousness at
this moment. Rather you are alert, and your senses are
clear. Your mind is deeply calm, and you have forgotten
about yourself. But as previously noted, it may be only
for two or three seconds that you are in meditation.

The moment of meditation is often very short
initially, but it will come to last longer. Even then, our
senses continue to function, and some perceptions
relating to sensory impressions will still arise one after
another. This is natural for the human mind. What
is important is that you do not respond to what you
perceive during the meditation period. Don't become
attached to any thought or feeling which turns up, even
though you are sensing it. Just do nothing and let these
thoughts go. Once you get the feeling of doing nothing
during meditation, what you perceive will not create an
endless chain of thoughts.

Profound and Ongoing Changes

Sometimes even a practitioner who has meditated
for numerous years will only be in a deep state of

meditation for a few minutes, even if he or she sits for 30 minutes. But don't imagine that these several minutes are not valuable and life altering. What is important is the depth, not the length, of meditation. Equally important is your capacity to notice the true nature of the absolute stillness that you fall into during meditation. However brief the interlude of meditation is, it has great effect on the meditator. Often this condition of deep calmness will spontaneously arise again during a crisis or when facing some important moment.

With ongoing meditation training, however, you will be able to enter muga munen at will. This is useful whenever you come across a very serious life problem or when you are faced with a dilemma that you can't immediately find an answer to. At these times, try sitting in meditation, forgetting yourself, and staying calmly alert in the present. During the period of sitting and doing nothing, don't be surprised if a good idea or sudden inspiration pops up inside you that will resolve your problem. Such spontaneous realizations often take place when we settle ourselves, which lets the mind, especially its unconscious aspect, work more efficiently.

The subconscious acts as a storeroom for our past experiences, with the elements housed in the subconscious forming the conscious mind. That which we repeat daily becomes part of the subconscious in

the form of a habit. After you have practiced meditation for several years, muga munen will stay in your
subconscious 24 hours a day, giving you vast mental
strength. I believe our lives can be completely changed
by meditation, causing us to live in a higher dimension
and in a more evolved way. There we can find great joy,
peace, and freedom.

Chapter 2

ANJO DAZA HO: SONIC MEDITATION

Before I present another method of concentration leading to meditation, I would like to further explain the difference between muga ichi-nen (concentration) and muga munen (meditation), because these two Japanese terms are essential keys to understanding what meditation is. Concentration and meditation are so similar that they are often mistakenly thought of as being the same. The "high," or ecstatic feeling, which we have when we concentrate on one thing we like, while forgetting about ourselves, is thought by some to be a kind of meditation. For example, a person who enjoys jogging and experiences a "running high" might say, "I don't need meditation. My meditation is jogging. That's enough."

But that isn't the sort of meditation being outlined in this book. Certainly jogging can be practiced so that it leads to deep levels of concentration, in which the mind is fully in tune with the moment and the physical movement that is taking place. One can be "in the zone," and for lots of people this is beneficial. However, the meditation I'm about to clarify is different from this.

To make this difference clear, I think it will be useful to examine some idioms, composed of Japanese characters, to put in plain words the difference between concentration and meditation. These idioms are short, compact, and clearly express the distinction and relationship between concentration and meditation. They originally came from Chinese Zen meditation.

Defining What is Beyond Definition: Muga Ichi-nen and Muga Munen

As you now realize, muga means literally "no self," but it can also imply a state of no attachments, and this is generally all most Japanese dictionaries will tell you. But I want to give you more to go on.

The ga of muga has two meanings:

1. Self (but not our real eternal self, rather our visible and impermanent self)

2. Attachment or obsession

46

The mu of muga is a prefix denoting the lack or absence of something, similar to "un-," "dis-," or "non-" in English. Most translators have translated muga into "no self" almost automatically, without thinking deeply about the profound implications of this term. But in Zen meditation, the "self" referred to (in the ga of) muga is not our real self. In the Zen sense, muga refers to a false, transient self that's connected to the phenomenal world. So, perhaps a truer definition would be that muga is to transcend our ephemeral self to realize a genuine self that exists beyond attachment to the impermanent aspects of life. True, this is a rather lengthy definition, but it is also one that makes muga clearer, especially to non-Japanese speaking people. Muga can be achieved by freeing ourselves from distracting thoughts, inhibitions, and attachments to transient things, thus allowing us to perceive what lies beyond such things: our true and undying self.

Ichi-nen means "one thought," and in the context of meditation, it implies concentrating on one object. Therefore, muga ichi-nen is the state of the mind in which we realize our real being, transcending what we often think of as our self, while focusing our attention on one thing. In short, muga ichi-nen is the real self that is paying attention to one thought or to the present moment.

In order to fully understand the immense implications of this concept, we first must recognize that we are often distracted by irrelevant (or needless) thoughts that prevent us from clearly perceiving life as it really is, life at this moment. That is, the mind is often scattered, wandering from one object to another, from one thought to another. Then we are inclined to lose sight of our actual nature, solely relating to aspects of ourselves that are as impermanent and transitory as our coming and going thoughts. This is what I call the false self, which we transcend in the state of muga.

We tend to become attached to, or even obsessed with, these chaotic thoughts. The more strongly we are attached to certain things or ideas, the more we agonize over these things in life. We suffer when we cling to that which is temporary. We can't truly have it, control it, or hang on to it—whether "it" is an idea, a person, or a possession. And it can be very difficult to get out of this state, once we are fully immersed in our obsessions and attachments, as those complexes stick to the mind and do not allow us to have clear consciousness. They often create such stress that we're unable to concentrate well on anything.

So, muga ichi-nen is essentially concentration, but as you can see from what I've just written, the term has a deep meaning that goes further than what we typically think of as "just concentration." On the other hand, meditation can be explained as the state of mind called muga munen.

You now know how I define muga. And you have also read that munen means "no thoughts," and it suggests being beyond distractions. Munen is a mind without mental wandering—a pure, clear mind, which is like the surface of a calm lake that reflects everything clearly. This lake, and the mind in muga munen, is like a polished mirror that reveals objects precisely as they really are. Munen is a positive, strong mind that's free from inhibitions. And while muga munen is literally "no self, no thoughts," it can be more easily interpreted as identification with our real self while existing beyond attachments to thought and transcending inhibitions.

One Consecutive Stream of Sound: Sonic Meditation

Concentration must precede meditation. In turn, as we enter into meditation, we have a chance to see into our real nature and the genuine nature of existence. Concurrently, meditation can enhance our ability to pay attention, heighten willpower, and evoke profound tranquility. Blood pressure drops, pulse rate slows, breathing becomes calmer and deeper, and realizing these byproducts of meditation may be why you purchased this book. So how can we arrive at a level of concentration intense enough to throw off distracting thoughts?

The answer is straightforward, but not necessarily easy. You have read about using a visual point of focus as a device that leads to concentration, but you can also listen to one consecutive stream of sound. This is a simple means to arrive at effective concentration, the state of muga ichi-nen. You can then naturally enter the state of meditation, the state of muga munen. Nakamura Sensei called this technique *Anjo Daza Ho*, literally "A Method of Sitting Peacefully." I sometimes refer to this method as sonic meditation.

In my experience, some sounds are easier to use than others for meditation. Music and birds singing are not so effective in concentration-meditation, because music and bird songs tend to arouse sensations or feelings, and do not easily lead you to muga munen.

Step One:
Listen to a Single Sound and Forget Yourself

One sound I recommend is that of a buzzer, something like a doorbell buzzer or an alarm clock buzzer. Nakamura Sensei, advocated using this sharp, attention-grabbing sound in his book *Seidai na Jinsei*. Nakamura Sensei studied yoga in India, and some Indian yoga teachers predated him in explaining the use of "a stream-like, continuing sound" as an object of concentration for meditation. But not everyone teaching meditation based around sound has concretely explained how to effectively concentrate on this stream-like, continuing sound. The hum of a buzzer is the kind of tone that's sharp enough to hold the mind's attention.

Step Two:
Drop the Sound and Listen to Nothingness

Gently close your eyes, listen to the buzzer intently, and try to forget anything else. Once the mind is concentrated so deeply on this hum that only one thought is present (the buzzing), we arrive at muga ichi-nen. At this point, the sound should cut off. And when the sound is no longer heard, continue to concentrate but listen to the nothingness. Using this method of sonic meditation, you can fall into muga munen, the state of forgetting about yourself or attachments, while transcending thought.

In Japan, your assistant or your teacher will switch off the buzzer for you. Unfortunately, these buzzers

(**Figure 7**) are not commercially available, and follow-ers of Anjo Daza Ho usually build them. Moreover, if you want to practice this method alone, you not only have to build a buzzer, but you have to construct one with a timer, which produces a sound for 30 to 60 seconds and suddenly goes off automatically. The easiest way around this is to purchase the meditation CD produced by my friends at the Sennin Foundation Center for Japanese Cultural Arts in California. Their CD contains appropriate sounds for sonic meditation, with correct intervals of time between the sounds for sitting in meditative silence. You can order their CD at www.senninfoundation.com.

FIGURE 7: *Softly close your eyes. Let the sound of the buzzer fill your mind to form one thought and forget your transient self. When the sound switches off, continue to concentrate, listening to nothingness in a state that's not attached to your body or your thoughts.*

You can also record the sound of an electric shaver in place of a buzzer. If you are a musician, you can produce a sound like that of a buzzer with a violin, cello, or viola with the same pitch (tune, frequency), record it to a CD, and use it for concentration-meditation practice.

Nakamura Sensei told me:

> The silence (you hear when the buzzer ceases) is the true character of the universe, and you receive the energy of the absolute universe in the silence. At first, you may feel deep stillness for only one or two seconds when the buzzer stops. But the length of time you feel this stillness will last longer as you continue practicing.

When you are listening to the buzzer, you are concentrating in the state of muga ichi-nen, and when the resonance turns off, deep calmness visits you. That is meditation, or muga munen.

A Rin Bell is Useful for Sonic Meditation

You can also use the ringing of a Japanese *rin* bell as the object of concentration in meditation (**Figure 8**). You can buy these bowl-shaped bells at many stores selling Buddhist altars and other spiritual goods in

Japan or Asia. In the West, they may be a bit harder to purchase, but the aforementioned audio CD from the Sennin Foundation Center contains the sound of this bell as well as a buzzer's resonance, and this is a useful alternative to actually buying a Japanese meditation bell.

These bells come with a wooden striker. One merely hits the edge of the bell to produce a peaceful tone. A rin (a.k.a. *kane*) that rings longer is recommended, but at the first stage of your practice, any rin will work. The sound of a rin lasts 20 to 30 seconds on average, but some good quality rin, alloyed with first-rate metals, will ring more than a minute. A rin whose sound is shorter than 20 seconds is less ideal.

FIGURE 8: *This bell is called rin or kane. With your eyes softly closed, focus on it's declining tone to realize "no self, one thought." As the sound lessens, brain waves grow calmer. Keep pursuing this infinitely fading note to achieve a state beyond your ephemeral self and all thoughts. Then, sit and do nothing.*

Concerning the use of the rin for concentration-meditation practice, Nakamura Sensei explained to me:

As the reverberating sound of a rin bell gradually fades away, you can feel muga ichi-nen, and then muga munen, which is true meditation. It is desirable for you to become a person who can jump into the state of muga munen any time in your life.

Nakamura Tempu-style meditation can actually be explained in this short paragraph, but it is a revolutionary method in the human history of meditation. It seems so simple and easy that some people may readily dismiss it, so be careful in evaluating the method.

How can you evaluate sonic meditation? There is only one reliable way to appraise anything—direct and personal experience. Make a habit of listening to a sound for concentration-meditation for 20 to 30 minutes every day. You can use the buzzer or the bell as the focal point of your concentration, or you can alternate between these two sounds (as on the Sennin Foundation Center's CD). But you must practice daily to learn to concentrate so fully on a given sound that it fills your entire mind, releasing self-consciousness. Subsequently, continue to listen and concentrate as the resonance fades, until you are listening to nothingness itself. Then simply sit in stillness and silence. If you grow distracted, you can hit the bell and start over anytime or wait for the sound to repeat on the CD. Over time, you'll discover the effectiveness of this uncomplicated method of meditation and be thankful for its benefits.

When Thoughts Attack

Many people who try meditation complain, "When I learned meditation the teacher told me not to think of anything, but countless thoughts, one after another, attacked me. I found it very difficult to stop thinking." This is a common problem, but if you ring your bell at the moment you're distracted by a chain of needless thoughts, your concentration on the new reverberation instantly breaks this chain and allows the basic state of calm concentration to continue.

There's no need to struggle with unwanted distractions in meditation, just hit the bell again and start over whenever thoughts come up, especially if you're a beginner. It's acceptable to listen to the bell numerous times in one session of meditative practice. Some Zen priests, who have numerous years of training, say they can eliminate all thoughts if they sit still for at least half an hour or one hour. But ordinary meditators will initially find it difficult to make the mind empty, as they often feel pain or an itching sensation somewhere in their body, causing various thoughts to rise up.

This is the key point—whenever a disturbing idea turns up in your mind, ring the bell once more, listen to it, and let the sound fill your mind instead of whatever was distracting you. Then, follow this sound again into nothingness, which allows you to feel deep tranquility.

The experience of empty consciousness, even if only for a few seconds, is of great value and shouldn't be taken for granted. Even if you have to start over multiple times in one meditation session, each of these experiences of muga munen accumulate in the subconscious, and the subconscious mind streams into and greatly affects your conscious mental state and activities. When we experience a state beyond self and beyond thought, this condition of great calmness penetrates the subconscious, reorienting our unconscious mind toward calmness. Over time, it will have a real impact on your everyday life, allowing you to stay calm in situations that would have upset you before.

Perhaps the biggest problem beginners face is thinking about not thinking during meditation. For instance, if you think while meditating, "Oh, a thought came up again. This is no good. I must try to think nothing," you are thinking about not thinking. That breaks meditation.

As you grow accustomed to the practice, you'll find that any thought will be gone in short order. Thoughts have no permanent reality of their own. We sustain them by mentally commenting on them or by trying to make them go away. So if some thought or physical sensation comes up, just notice it without cerebral commentary, and do nothing. It will dissolve, and eventually you'll realize how to not be attached to thought, which is a key to mastering meditation. If you have mastered meditation, you will find it possible to return to absolute stillness, or muga munen, even after engaging in thought. As you develop this skill, you will not need to ring your bell each time a thought arises.

Nakamura Sensei on one occasion told us:

> Once in a while a negative idea or feeling comes up in my mind. At these times, I may lean against a pillar and listen deeply to some sound around me and put my mind in the state of no attachment, no obsession. At this moment, the negativity leaves me and often inspiration visits me. This inspiration allows me to resolve any problem in a positive direction.

The clarity of mind produced by real meditation allows us to see and feel everything clearly, which in turn gives rise to inspiration and creative responses. I know numerous scholars and businessmen, who succeeded in their projects by getting inspiration or good ideas after practicing Anjo Daza Ho. They are all marvelously strong in health and mental abilities.

Do Not Try to Meditate, but Try to Concentrate

At first, spend more time listening to the rin or buzzer with one-pointed concentration than trying to meditate. Concentration must precede meditation, and it is not something to be glossed over. Just listening to a sound and concentrating is meaningful, because you can experience muga and throw away needless thoughts. And although muga ichi-nen is the first step in meditation, it also produces exceptional levels of calmness and relaxation. In essence, by concentrating on something, instead of worrying about our problems and ourselves, we experience a psychological vacation that greatly benefits our mental and physical health.

Once you feel comfortable concentrating on a single sound without mentally wavering, then you can gradually make the time for meditation longer. Only two or three minutes of meditation out of 20 minutes of practice can still effectively produce deeper serenity and relaxation. Nakamura Sensei often told me, "Just two or three seconds of meditation has value."

Do not try hard to meditate or experience muga munen; this must happen of its own accord. Try hard to concentrate on the bell and/or the buzzer. If you realize superior concentration, you will naturally experience meditation as the sound fades, and this experience takes place without effort. It is ironic that if you try to stop thinking, you'll find yourself thinking, "I must stop thinking." The knack of sonic meditation is in being one, or united, with the sound. The intensity of concentration, which is most important, decides the depth of meditation, as meditation is an outgrowth of attention being fixed in the present moment, the only moment that is real.

When we begin to listen to a buzzer or a rin, our brain waves become calmer and longer, with fewer fluctuations, until they produce alpha waves when we enter meditation. When we experience sudden inspiration or hit upon a good idea, alpha waves are active in the brain. In addition, I believe that meditation gives us deeper rest than sleep.

I feel life energy, which we call ki in Japan, arises from the depths of the subconscious during meditative practice. Many people are inclined to think our strength comes solely from substances outside ourselves such as food, nutritious supplements, air, and sunshine. Indeed these are sources of life energy, or ki, and they're needed to support life, but essential life energy also lies deep in our mind. Through meditation, we can discover and merge with ki, the source of all life, and this gives us a greater energy and power to deal with events in our lives.

An Alternative Sound

I think a rin bell is the easiest tool to use for concentration in Anjo Daza Ho. It is the handiest, and you can ring it as often as you like, with intervals you choose. As mentioned earlier, the buzzer works best on an audio CD or in a group meditation, with a leader switching it off without warning. Plus, we may develop more intense concentration by listening to a fainter sound that gradually fades away versus the louder sound of the buzzer. On the other hand, the more penetrating buzzer is rather good for a beginner, since it drowns out various distracting ambient noises. When it clicks off, the subsequent hush is intense, making it a bit easier for beginners to catch the feeling of deep silence, or muga munen.

But there is another alternative. It is a Tibetan bowl (or singing bowl), which is used by Buddhist priests in Tibet to calm the mind. The sound is attractive and mysterious, with a low soft reverberation that lasts a long time.

You can get a Tibetan bowl at shops selling Indian or Asian handicrafts or folk arts. A handmade bowl, which is not mass-produced, can be expensive but it is often of high quality and produces a fine sound.

It takes some time for you to get accustomed to the way of ringing the bowl. You do not hit it with a wooden stick like the rin, but rub (scrape) along the outside of the circular upper rim. You have to rub it firmly and slowly with the stick never parting from the rim. If you rub it about three times around the rim well, you'll hear the sound of the bell.

Even though most Tibetan and Nepali people hold the bowl in their left hand to absorb the vibration, I suggest putting the bowl on a cushion, so that you can hold your hands together as in **Figure 9**. Nakamura Sensei felt crossing hands together in this mudra, or gesture, makes concentration more intense. You can also place your hands palm up on your knees, forming rings with the thumbs and index fingers, like the photo of me on the cover of this book. This mudra is common in Indian yoga.

At temples in Nepal, Tibet, and India, a Tibetan bowl is used as a musical instrument, and it is believed the sound has a healing power. Even some doctors, like Mitchell L. Gaynor, a leading oncologist in the U. S., are said to have medically acknowledged the bell's power for helping to cure illness. [4]

You can use the tone of a buzzer, a Japanese rin bell, or a Tibetan singing bowl as a point of auditory focus. You can use a dot as point of visual focus. But it is important to concentrate the mind deeply each day on one point, which can lead to the cultivation of remarkable willpower and attention.

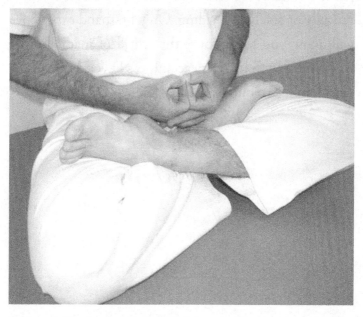

FIGURE 9: *This hand position is called Sorin-in. Form rings with the index fingers and thumbs. Interlace the other fingers and keep the palms up. Place your hands close to the body and below the navel.*

Then once your mind is focused on the dot, close your eyes and watch the image gradually fade into noth-ingness; your brain waves will also gradually become calmer as they move on a never-ending path toward emptiness. Or listen to a sound with one-pointed focus, and follow the tone as it gradually decreases, moving toward stillness and silence, without losing the state of attention.

Either approach will work, but they must be put into practice daily. The act of meditating is the main point of this book, and it cannot be understood theo-retically or solely by reading. Only firsthand experience will allow you to discover the world of meditation, a world filled with ki and peacefulness beyond thought, a world linked to our real self.

Chapter 3

WHAT IS MEDITATION?

Nakamura Tempu Sensei is widely known in Japan for his innovative meditation instruction and his great awareness of human nature. He often said to us during lectures on meditation, "A human being is strongest when in the state of muga munen." It seems to me that grasping this truth is an essential part of human existence.

We are psychologically most effective, efficient, and powerful when we are meditating, and more and more science is proving this idea. We possess in the depths of our minds a remarkable ability, which allows us to unite with the infinite power of the universe, which as mentioned earlier, Japanese people call ki. Everyone has ki, but for many it remains an immense latent power. But ki can be discovered and cultivated by calming the mind via meditation, eventually realizing how to sustain this calmness under all circumstances. Since ki is the animating force of nature, our capacity to connect with it is natural and innate, always waiting within our subconscious and ready to enhance every aspect of our lives. Meditation can unlock this hidden potential.

Countless yoga meditators, Zen priests, and philosophers have discussed the question of what meditation is in different ways, as it is a subject that has numerous dimensions. In this chapter, I'll introduce some leading figures in meditation and use their ideas to explore the various elements of meditation. Several of these individuals are (or were) great teachers of Zen and yoga, although you might not be familiar with all of them. Their teachings may help you understand meditation more fully and encourage you to practice the concentration-meditation outlined in prior chapters.

Meditative Consciousness

Muga munen consciousness during true meditation is neither that of sleeping nor dreaming. Of course, it is not the usual consciousness that lots of people have when they are awake either, but it is also not something unnatural or a condition we have never experienced before. Actually, all of us experience meditative consciousness once in a while in everyday life, some-times without fully realizing what has just occurred.

We enter a kind of meditation when the mind is wholly absorbed in the moment. For example, if we unexpectedly see something uniquely beautiful or unusual, the mind is suddenly fully awake and in the present moment, just like in the forms of meditation discussed in prior chapters. We are not thinking about the past or the future. We are just "there," completely immersed in the instant, in a state beyond time, beyond thought, beyond self-consciousness.

This usually doesn't take place deliberately; it is often an unconscious response that evokes a condition akin to muga munen. Even when listening to a fascinat-ing lecture, if the speaker abruptly pauses ... we may involuntarily enter meditation for a second or so. But this might only last for a moment, and we frequently fail to grasp the significance of what just happened—precisely because it took place suddenly and without premeditation.

Yet oftentimes exceptionally talented people—great artists, musicians, or inventors who discover or create something epoch-making for humanity—spontane-ously and unconsciously enter the state of meditation without effort. It is at these instants that they make profound discoveries and give birth to great art.

A Nobel Prize Winner's Experience

Professor Masakawa Hidetoshi, who won a Nobel Prize in physics in 2008, is one of my colleagues at Kyoto Sangyo University. He discovered something revolutionary about the structure of the elementary particle, and he told me how he unexpectedly hit upon this new theory. He actually got the idea when resting in a hot bath at home.

He was intensely concentrating on a theoretical physics problem in his office at our university, but he was getting nowhere—until he relaxed completely in the bathtub. The deep concentration on his research at work focused his mind fully; similar to the way we focus the mind on one sound or one visual point in meditation. When he totally relaxed in the bath—doing and thinking nothing—he spontaneously experienced meditative consciousness akin to the moment that we realize objectless concentration in meditation. In this instant he broke through the barriers that had been troubling him, discovering something wholly new and unforeseen.

Moteki Kenichiro, a well-known brain scientist in Japan, says "pure experience," which occurs in childhood when we see or hear innocently and with curiosity, is similar to meditation. He also says a child can briefly enter into meditation when hiding in the bushes with a net to catch a butterfly, because his/her mind is absolutely calm (muga munen) at that moment. I agree, and these concepts are useful for understanding what meditation is: a very natural state of the mind. It is this mental state that some psychologists call "pure consciousness," and I call muga munen, the condition of thinking and doing nothing.

As we get older, we tend to be preoccupied with endless matters that worry us, always thinking about this and that. And it becomes difficult to rest the mind, to experience muga munen. Meditation is just allowing the mind to return to its natural resting state; it is not a special and unknown domain that's only attainable through harsh ascetic practice.

The Search for True Meditation

Seemingly from the beginning of time, people have struggled to discover real meditation. Christian monks, Indian yogis, Zen priests, and innumerable others have sought unity with the actual nature of the universe, striving to grasp their true self by meditating. But many of them failed in their endeavor, unable to find the path to deep concentration, which leads to meditation. Only a few reached the state of genuine meditation, and they came to be called saints, sages, and gurus.

Reaching concentration, or muga ichi-nen, needn't be a complex matter; just focus your attention on an object or be absorbed in what you like to do. However, to reach muga munen you need to practice something more like the methods of concentration-meditation I have introduced.

Historically, religions have provided methods of attaining muga ichi-nen, forgetting about the impermanent self to eliminate the mind's wandering. Christianity, for instance, teaches to pray earnestly. In fact, followers of any religion can be in muga ichi-nen when praying, thus eliminating mental distractions and calming the mind. Buddhists are also in muga ichi-nen when they recite *mantra*, sacred words repeated mentally or verbally again and again. But not everyone wants to join a specific religion to learn meditation, and even for such people, distracting thoughts may still remain in their minds, making it difficult to reach muga munen. This is one of the reasons I wrote this book; I want to provide the public, especially in the West, with simple and effective meditation methods that aren't tied to any particular religion.

In yoga and Zen, people also searched for the method to attain muga munen, which lies deeper in the mind than muga ichi-nen. Some succeeded.

Dogen and Meditation

Dogen (1200-1253), a famous Zen priest in 13th century Japan, was an unusual person who reached the condition of muga munen. He expressed meditation as *jin shin datsu raku*. This is literally, "body and mind fall away," which means forgetting about both mind and body—muga munen.

Dogen explained that meditation is "departing from obsessions and attachments to ephemeral things," and "eliminating mental complexes." What he meant was that in meditation the condition of muga munen could be achieved by throwing away attachments and self-centered ideas. The mind's mirror is clouded by such needless thoughts, and meditation should figuratively clean this mirror, which can then reflect the truths of the universe and the practitioner's true self. [5]

Perhaps the most well known Zen philosopher in Japan, Dogen studied in China with the distinguished Zen priest Nyo Jyo and realized enlightenment at the age of 26. He is said to have reached this status through esoteric sitting meditation. As a result, a great number of people who think seriously about human life and meditation—in the USA, Europe, and Japan—have read Dogen's works. A well-respected author of Zen literature, he often wrote about the feeling of meditation using unique poetic similes, which makes his books difficult to understand. Since my writing style is different from this, I hope that this small book will make it easier for Dogen fans to grasp the meaning behind his metaphors.

He was born from parents of top-ranking noble families, and he could have become *kampaku* ("prime minister") if he had desired. His father died when he was three years old, and his mother passed away when he was eight, which made him think about life and death seriously. He was so intelligent that he read scriptures and books on Buddhism even in his childhood. He made a sudden decision at 14 to leave home, climb Mt. Hiei east of Kyoto, and visit his uncle, a Buddhist priest living at a temple deep in the mountains. He never looked back.

Dogen is said to have had an austere dignity like that of a great statesman or an ancient *samurai*. But he wasn't interested in politics or military matters, and he studied Zen Buddhism, deeply devoting himself to searching for the truths of life. In his time, the majority of Zen priests wrote exclusively in Chinese, making it difficult for normal Japanese people to read their teachings. Dogen, however, wrote Zen books in Japanese so ordinary people might read them.

Since he was a talented poet, this probably explains

why his writings have so many poetically metaphoric phrases, and his lyrical form of writing seems to attract today's intellectually oriented readers all the more for its difficulty. Numerous novelists, poets, and religious people have tried to interpret his unique expressions, which are so hard for average folks to understand. And every year there are more books published on his philosophical ideas and religious teachings, in Japanese and other languages. Nonetheless, I'm not convinced that very many more readers are actually realizing the meaning of meditation through these volumes.

I have also been inspired by Dogen's Zen musings (as was Nakamura Sensei). His influence can be felt in both Nakamura Sensei's writings and this book. But we aren't the only people that have created a simpler interpretation of Dogen's meditation teachings.

Professor Tamaki and Dogen

There are scores of researchers writing about Dogen in Japan, but I feel the most remarkable author among them is Tamaki Koshiro Sensei, Professor Emeritus of Tokyo University in religious studies. His excellent essays simply explain how Dogen practiced *zazen*, "Zen sitting meditation," and reached a high level of spiritual consciousness.

Tamaki Sensei describes Dogen's meditation as "unified body and mind" or "unification of mind and body." He regards coordination of mind and body as the ideal state for human beings, exactly the same as what Nakamura Sensei taught. In meditation, the mind is concentrating, meaning the mind is in the present moment. Since the body can only exist in the present, during meditation mind and body are united as one. This oneness of mind and body allows us to bring forth our full, integrated potential (as opposed to manifesting the strength of just the mind or body independently). It also amounts to a condition in which every part of us exists in harmony with every other part.

Tamaki Sensei also mentions Dogen's assertion that meditation is "eternal in time, universal in space" and Dogen's reference to "holding all the things in the cosmos in both hands." In the previously described forms of meditation, we concentrated the mind deeply on one point or one sound, and this brought the mind into the present. This present is the only reality; past and future do not exist except as ideas. Reality is now.

Time is an artificial construct; although sometimes useful, it's ultimately unreal. It involves a progression from the past to the future, but really there is no ultimate distinction between past, present, and future. In meditation, we learn how to rest peacefully in the present, discovering that the moment transcends any movement in time, making it eternal—"eternal in time, universal in space."[6]

"Universal in space" and "holding the cosmos in both hands" generally refer to the realization of our innate unity with the universe. Returning again to the aforementioned two forms of meditation, when we give attention to one sound or one point, we merge with the object of concentration. When we forget ourselves, the distinction between the listener and the sound, the observer and the observed, dissolves into oneness. When "we" are not there, the artificial, self-constructed barriers between us and the totality of existence drop away.

Professor Tamaki didn't teach meditation to the general public, but he did attain the deepest state of meditation and wrote a number of useful, enlightening books on numerous difficult subjects such as Zen, yoga, Christianity, Western philosophy, and others. What's more, he mastered Greek, Latin, and classical Chinese, not to mention English, French, and German, allowing him read the original writings of the world's major philosophers, thinkers, and religious teachers. Tamaki Sensei was also one of a small number of Japanese researchers who could read and interpret the Pali language, in which the oldest and original teachings of Buddha are recorded.

Tamaki Sensei insisted anyone can reach the same deep realization as the historical Buddha and experience what he did, but only if we meditate properly. According to Professor Tamaki, as a result of meditation our doubts about life will be gone, and in his books he has indicated that meditation is the path to eternity and also is the eternal path for us to walk on. He explains that functioning with a unified mind and body was observed in at least some people all over the world in ancient times, but today the importance of mind and body unification via meditation seems to be more recognized by people interested in Indian thought, yoga, and Zen.

Tamaki Sensei also states that meditating can alleviate chronic fatigue, even that which cannot be cured by sleeping. He meditated often in order to recover from exhaustion. (According to Hirai Tomio's book *Zazen no Kagaku*, some Japanese medical studies of brain waves show meditation gives us deeper rest than sleep does, affirming Tamaki Sensei's assertion.) Professor Tamaki also frankly wrote in his books that meditation saved him from craziness—the bottom of despair where dark and light interlace. He remembered sitting in meditation before he slipped into his bed, stealthily avoiding the strict regulations of the Japanese Imperial Army, when he served during World War II.

It was meditation that helped him through war, an experience that no sane person—on either side—wants to undergo.

In *Tozai Shiso no Kontei ni Aru Mono* ("What Lies at the Bottom of Western and Eastern Thoughts") he explained:

> We can vividly sense the same universal life that ancient people thousand of years ago discovered in meditation. Meditation is a wonderful vein in history, in which modern man can share a common experience with his ancient ancestors, an experience that is not dependent on words. Buddha and Dogen shared the purpose and method of meditation, even though they lived 1500 years apart.[7]

Again, he was affirming that meditation is the realization of a moment beyond time and a condition of unity with all creations. Tamaki Sensei's explanations of meditation are important, and since most Westerners are not familiar with his writings, I wanted to give you his take on aspects of this subject. Unity of mind and body, union with the universe, and transcending time to sense the ultimate reality of life are all essential points for meditators to consider.

Sahota Tsuruji, Yoga Researcher

Professor Sahota Tsuruji is another important Japanese scholar, who studied and practiced yoga/meditation. He wrote several books on it, which are useful, enlightening, and reliable. He described meditation as: "sustained calm and clear consciousness," and wrote in *Yoga Konpon Kyoten*, "When we meditate, the content of thinking broadens." [8]

"The content of thinking broadens" is similar to Nakamura Sensei's oft-used phrase "*reiseishin* arises." Reiseishin is literally "spiritual mind" or "spiritual consciousness." Nakamura Sensei taught that the existence of reiseishin in our mind is often hidden by mental agitation, but it arises when we meditate and calm the mind. When the psyche is deeply still, we can perceive our reiseishin, which allows us to more effectively and intuitively make decisions in life.

Students of Nakamura Sensei often noticed that during meditation they felt suddenly inspired to attempt a new direction in life, or that during meditation they would discover an answer to a long standing problem. Such sudden inspiration and realization is the work of reiseishin, which allows us to act spontaneously in a way that is not solely dependent on either emotion or reason. With the manifestation of reiseishin comes a new, instinctive, and profoundly more effective means of judging what direction to take in life.

Sahota Sensei studied European philosophy at Kyoto University and became a professor of philosophy at Ritsumeikan University and Osaka University. He practiced yoga in India and translated the works of Patanjali, a celebrated ancient yoga adept, who edited the famous authoritative text, *The Yoga Sutras*. Compiled in the fifth century, it is the classic literature read in India by yoga students. In this book, Patanjali defined meditation as, "a current of unified thought." "Unified thought" means "thinking in a state of mind and body unification." In meditation, both the mind and body concentrate calmly in the present moment: they are in the same place at the same time. In this sense, they are unified. Along the same lines, concentration is the consolidation of attention—"a current of unified thought"—that leads to meditation.

Patanjali lived long ago in India. In modern times, there was one person that can be thought of as the Patanjali of Japan: Nakamura Tempu Sensei.

Nakamura Tempu, The Great Meditator

Nakamura Sensei (1876-1968) had a dramatic and fascinating life. In his early years, he contracted tuberculosis and was given a few months to live. He launched a global quest to, if not cure his tuberculosis, at least learn how to face his own death. This search first took him to the USA, where he studied medicine at Columbia University.

Next, he traveled to Europe, where he lived with actress Sarah Bernhardt and researched psychology. In Egypt he encountered Kaliapa (a.k.a. Kaliappa), an Indian mystic and yoga master, who brought him to India for a final attempt to save his life. After austere meditation in the Himalayas, Nakamura Sensei attained enlightenment, shook off the bonds of illness, and returned to Japan a changed man.

He taught Shin-shin-toitsu-do ("The Way of Mind and Body Unification") for over 50 years and authored bestselling books. He trained over 100,000 people, including members of the Japanese Imperial Family, government officials, business leaders, top athletes, celebrated actors, martial arts experts, and notable novelists. As you have read, he was my primary teacher.

Nakamura Sensei (**Figure 10**) wasn't an eminent scholar or academic, like Professors Sahota or Tamaki, but in the eyes of many, he was a far greater practitioner of yoga and meditation. Actually, for some Japanese meditators, including myself, he was the best teacher of pragmatic yoga methods we've ever had in Japan. He

FIGURE 10: *Nakamura Tempu Sensei was the founder of a style of Japanese yoga and meditation called Shin-shin-toitsu-do. He is often thought of as the father of yoga in Japan.*

developed near superhuman abilities, strengthened his character, and was admired by numerous celebrated Japanese leaders in the realms of business, politics, religion, science, and other fields.

He discovered the methods of meditation that I wrote about earlier in this book. They are part of his system of Japanese yoga commonly known as *Shin-shin-toitsu-ho*, "The Method of Mind and Body Unification," or alternately *Shin-shin-toitsu-do*, "The Way of Mind and Body Unification." It is a meditative methodology that any person can practice; a system based on his unique life views that grew out of the unusual experiences of his stormy and eventful life. (I introduced Shin-shin-toitsu-ho in my Japanese book *Kokoro wo Ku ni Suru* in 2009. Westerners can read about Shin-shin-toitsu-ho in H. E. Davey Sensei's *Japanese Yoga: The Way of Dynamic Meditation*, the first book in English on this subject.)

Nakamura Sensei espoused a way of living based on meditation and a positive attitude, both of which have a deep impact on our health and potential. He taught that meditative calm can, and must, be realized in the midst of action *(do chu no sei)*. Perhaps his ultimate teaching is that via meditation we can rediscover our innate unity with the universe.

Immanuel Kant

Nakamura Sensei studied Raja yoga, the yoga of meditation, in India under the tutelage of Kaliapa. But before this, he traveled through the USA and Europe, where he investigated Western philosophy and psychology. A major influence on his teachings was a German philosopher named Immanuel Kant, who is well known for the difficulty of his writings. Kant's writings have also influenced me, and I feel that the most pragmatic side of his thought concludes that one should "Listen to and follow what your conscience tells you." When I told this to one of my friends, he was surprised and he objected, saying, "Is it so easy?"

The art of living is simple, but simple may not be easy. In fact, what I've discovered after more than 50 years of meditation is that it's almost impossible to hear what your conscience tells you if you don't know how to concentrate and meditate. It's only when the mind is deeply still and clear that we "hear" our conscience.

But for many the mind is typically clouded with anxiety and attachment to various thoughts, beliefs, and past experiences. Consequently, we can't think clearly, or perceive what our reiseishin, perhaps most simply rendered in English as our conscience, is telling us. This leads us to commit errors in life and suffer as the result. Meditation aims at stilling the mind and releasing our attachments, producing clarity of perception that lets us listen to our conscience and intuitively decide the right path for us to take, from moment to moment.

Meditation has no specific objective or image associated with it, but it puts us on the true road to serenity and clear consciousness. I would say that ultimately meditation is a way of listening to our reiseishin, a "spiritual consciousness" akin to one's conscience.

In this chapter I introduced several important teachers of meditation that have influenced my imparting of this art and thus this book as well. I haven't attempted to fully explain their ideas, recognizing that the description of something is never the thing being described. It is always an approximation.

So I've hinted at important ideas associated with meditation, and I hope that you'll discover the meaning of these great teachers' words and philosophies for yourself as you meditate. That said, I'll explain more about the worldview of Nakamura Sensei and other important teachers of meditation and philosophy as this book unfolds. All of us can be inspired by their wisdom, but each of us must discover the meaning of such teachings for ourselves via meditation.

Chapter 4

MEDITATION AND ITS BENEFITS

In some ways, the purposes of meditation are its benefits. I have already referred to some of them previously, but in this chapter I'd like us to examine this topic more closely and from different angles (or viewpoints). Meditation aids numerous aspects of our lives, and all the benefits brought about by meditative practice are a byproduct of its purposes. In short, when we fully realize the genuine meditative condition, we simultaneously experience the advantages of this state.

As noted earlier, people grow interested in meditation for various reasons, but generally these motives can be boiled down to two primary categories:

1. A pragmatic orientation

2. A philosophical (or spiritual) orientation

We'll examine both approaches and viewpoints shortly, but first let's further explore the historical roots of meditation.

The Emergence of Meditation

Since the ancient past, yoga practitioners and Zen Buddhists have keenly sought after the state of meditation. In the West, Christian monks and friars in monasteries also tried hard to meditate to realize the truths of existence. As the result, authors steeped in yoga, Zen, Buddhism, and other spiritual paths have written countless books about meditation. The general public, consequently, has sometimes come to view the purposes of meditation as solely religious in orientation. While meditation is valued by many religions, it is a mistake to imagine that meditation must be connected to a certain religion.

When ancient people tried to know the truths of life, the necessity of meditation and its calm clarity of perception were naturally recognized. I doubt the original discoverers of meditative consciousness were attempting to pursue or promote an organized religion. Rather, they came to realize through trial and error that when their minds grew serene enough to take on a mirror-like quality, the truths of life were reflected in this mirror. This reflective calmness is the condition of meditation, or muga munen.

Over time some of these meditative ancestors did go on to establish religions based on their experiences (or their students founded them later), and for many, meditation has subsequently taken on heavy religious overtones. Yet we can actually approach meditation from numerous perspectives, all of which are valid. For some meditation may be a form of religious practice, for others it may be deeply spiritual but not inevitably tied to a specific religion, and for still others, meditation can be enjoyed for its pragmatic benefits.

Recent psychological studies and research have uncovered new and ample practical benefits of meditation, meditation not so much as religion, but as a means of realizing the essential nature of the mind. But Erich Fromm, a well-known psychoanalyst in the U.S., reported as far back as 1960 in *Zen Buddhism and Psychoanalysis* that meditation is an effective remedy for neurotic diseases (or neurosis). These kinds of pragmatic benefits of meditation are important, especially when we reflect upon the mental condition of people living in stressful modern societies around the world. Revitalizing the immune system, lowering blood pressure, eliminating nervous tension, and resolving emotional issues are just a few of the down-to-earth advantages and reasons for meditating, and these benefits can be realized by people of every religious orientation (or lack thereof).

Meditation Advantages

Mental health is improved in countless ways via meditation; enhanced calmness, concentration, and willpower are just a few of the upsides of regular meditation. And deeper relaxation and calmness correlate to improved physical health as well, in that the mind influences the body.

Concurrently, as the mind grows more peaceful, and as we learn to experience thoughts and perceptions without clinging to them, some people find that their phobias and forms of neurosis are cured. Meditation is also a simple way to transform the way you deal with stress and to let go of what is worrying you. It can even be used to recover from shock in traumatic situations.

Plus, positive thinking becomes easier. With deeper calmness, we feel better, which leads to a more upbeat attitude. Optimism, in turn, has a wide-ranging impact on our overall psychological state and physical wellbeing, all of which has been confirmed by numerous doctors, psychologists, and coaches. But these pragmatic benefits aren't all we get from meditation.

From a spiritual perspective, meditation is a way to know your genuine self. As you become more in touch with your real being, you will tap into the source of all creativity, and find yourself spontaneously inspired to move in new directions in life, while you hit upon fresh and creative ideas. Moreover, you'll discover that your genuine self is none other than the universe itself, and with this we unearth the wisdom of the universe, what some have termed cosmic consciousness, spiritual realization, or satori.

All of this takes place via meditation because meditation is a process of seeing clearly into our real essence, which is inextricably linked to nature, or the universe. The same ki, "life energy," that animates nature animates us. Arteries and veins run in the body like rivers, and our hair grows like grass. We are a microcosm of the universe.

For this reason, we have access to the ki of the universe, giving us unlimited creativity, strength, and potential, all of which can be experienced firsthand through meditation. In light of this immense human potential, it saddens me that some people use sleeping pills and tranquilizers to calm their mind, which can have side effects impacting their health, robbing them of ki. Meditation has no side effects, and it can lead to profound peace and easier sleep. But this calmness is not a dead, withdrawn, or passive state. Actually, meditation enhances or revives mental and physical vitality (ki), as many practitioners have reported.

Meditation requires concentration, and the more we meditate, the more we cultivate concentration. This is similar to lifting a weight—the more you do it, the easier it gets to lift it the next time you try. This cultivated concentration equates to willpower and self-control, which makes it easier to keep the mind positive under all circumstances. And in my experience, when we realize our genuine self through meditation, arising with this spiritual realization are both willpower and a positive attitude.

When your business is in trouble, or when you learn you're suffering from a serious disease, it's easy to be discouraged, making it impossible to stay positive. Unfortunately, this is when you most need to be optimistic, and if you've been meditating regularly, you'll have a reserve of strength to deal with these types of hardships without experiencing a complete psychological collapse. This, in turn, can help you to find solutions to your business woes and help you to use your mind to boost the vigor of your body. The will to live is a very real thing, but not everyone knows how to find such will. Meditation is the first place to look, and I'm not the only one saying this.

American inspirational writers and speakers advocated the importance of positive thinking for success in life as far back as prior to World War II. One of them, Napoleon Hill, also pointed out the importance of meditation for positive thinking. However, Hill, Dale Carnegie, and other advocates of positive thought didn't always offer simple and clear forms of meditation to support their programs of positivity. Although inspirational books and positive affirmations are useful in life, meditation is still essential for discovering how to live well, how to live positively.

Existential Crisis

Why am I living this life at all?

Simply trying to think our way out of an existential crisis doesn't work. These types of life problems baffle even philosophy majors and the most educated psychologists.

Meditation, in many ways, is simply being in a condition of mind and body unity. In meditation, we still the mind, while we bring it into the present moment, in sync with the body. In mind and body unification, or self-harmony, we enter into a state beyond linear thought, even beyond our five senses.

This is not to say that we are no longer capable of thinking. Meditative calmness actually makes it easier to think effectively. And I'm not suggesting that our basic senses no longer function during meditation; they are actually more acute. Meditation, however, is not limited to the conscious mind, to analytical thought, and to what our five senses perceive.

Meditation is not about thinking. Meditation is about experiencing.

It is an experience beyond definition, just as life is ultimately beyond defining. And it is the meditative experience that taps into the very essence of life, giving us a chance to sense our genuine nature and that of the universe.

No Past, No Future

Life, the universe, and our experience of living are always in the moment. This moment is the only true reality, but few of us spend much time there. Although this book isn't about traditional Zen meditation per se, Zen has several superior idioms relating to meditation that explain why the meditating mind must reside in the here and now.

One example is *zengo saidan*, which means literally "cutting down before and after." It really indicates forgetting about memories of the past and worries about the future. To set our mind in the immediate present is the aim of meditation, according to Zen philosophy. Most forms of genuine meditation espouse something similar.

Bad memories from the past and worries about the future tend to stick in our mind. It is hard to forget them sometimes. Even when we are working on something, they come up in our psyche and distract our concentration. If this becomes very serious, it can destroy our life in some way or another, leading to emotional inertia, mental disease, and even suicide. Fortunately, if we meditate for a relatively brief time every day, we may learn to reside in the present, freeing ourselves from those problems.

We feel guilt or regret about aspects of our past, which can't be changed. We experience anxiety about what may come in the future, but the future is unwritten. Yet when we keep the mind in the now, before and after disappear, along with our worries. This is a pragmatic benefit of meditation. Keeping the mind in the moment, unless we want to deliberately contemplate the past or future, also allows us to peer into the ultimate nature of life, which only exists at this instant. This is the major spiritual benefit of meditation.

Meditation is a Good Adviser

Although this may sound a bit odd, meditation actually gives you good advice, especially when you come to a crossroads in life and need to choose which way to go. Sometimes you cannot avoid choosing one route out of two (or sometimes more), yet you have no definite idea about what to do. This can result in you feeling puzzled and lost. Common crossroads in life involve choosing a school to enter, a job you really want to devote yourself to, or a partner you'd like to marry or live with. Even after finding a school to go to and a position to work in, you'll be forced to select this way or that way in your private life and at work throughout your life. To make a good decision, one you will not regret, turn to meditation.

You may think of consulting someone reliable, or a friend you trust, when you've lost your way in life. This can be helpful, but at the end of the day no one knows you as deeply as you're capable of knowing yourself. Even your close friends often perceive only their impressions of you, influenced by their own beliefs and biases, as much as they see the real you. So their advice may or may not be invariably reliable, fully considering your true nature. While getting general information and suggestions from others can be useful, meditation teaches to ultimately rely on yourself to find your way in life, because no matter how smart your advisers are, in the end it is your life and your decision.

But not everyone is willing to take responsibility for his or her life and live independently. Some people go to fortunetellers of one sort or another, while others rely on various superstitions and occult practices to make decisions. Be careful with this, because it can result in negating personal responsibility, suggesting that we can't rely on ourselves and learn directly from the universe (or life) without an intermediary to make the big choices for us. After a lifetime of meditation, this seems foolish to me. Those who know the method of meditation are free from these things.

The universe has given us a mind with unlimited potential and power, waiting to be unlocked. It is a mind directly connected to the universe, to the ultimate essence of reality. Turning away from this remarkable tool in favor of superstition is foolish; failing to make full and independent use of this gift is very unfortunate.

Meditate to Access the Universe

So when we come to a crossroads, requiring a decision that can't be easily resolved by looking at the available facts, turning to meditation lets us find the best path to take. This is especially true when we don't have many facts to work with, something most of us have encountered at points in our lives. At such a moment, sit in meditation and enter into muga munen, making no conscious attempt to find a solution to your problem. In this condition, we access our subconscious, and new, creative ideas may crop up unexpectedly as we meditate.

More than this, in muga munen we release our attachments to our relative, impermanent self, a self we typically think of as us. This removes the barrier between everything we imagine is us and everything we believe is not us. We merge with the universe, realizing that the mind sensing the universe isn't separate from the universe, that the observer is the observed.

In this condition, we may spontaneously feel that we need to do something, or an unanticipated idea may arise from the deep nothingness of muga munen. This is often the universe, which is really our genuine self, advising us. These unplanned eye-openers aren't based solely on emotion or reason, transcending both, and they've never led me down the wrong path. In meditation, we should listen to what our genuine self tells us, and then meditation will be of great help in living a life free from regrets. This is among the most important benefits of meditating.

A Unique Teacher of Japanese-style Yoga

Still another benefit of meditation lies in helping people. Serving others isn't something everyone thinks of when they imagine how meditation can aid them in life. Nevertheless, one of my teachers, Oki Masahiro Sensei, indicated in his *Meiso Yoga Nyumon* ("An Introduction to Meditation Yoga") that meditation cannot be fully grasped without serving other people. It is a unique way of understanding meditation, and the reason he established a yoga dojo in Mishima, Shizuoka. This dojo, or training hall, also has a beautiful view of Mt. Fuji, a gift from Oki Sensei to his students. Nakamura Sensei also taught the importance of helping others or creating something beneficial to people. Both of them shared the same idea, but what was unique about Oki Sensei, aside from his unusual personality, is the degree to which he united meditation with service to other people.

I visited Oki Sensei's dojo in 1971, three years after Nakamura Sensei passed away, and I briefly studied his version of yoga and meditation. One night he invited me to his room after supper. This was a rare honor, and he made a point of doing this after a very long day for him. We talked intimately for several hours, discussing life. All of a sudden he declared,

"You're a genius!" which surprised me. I didn't get his point then, but now I understand he was trying to encourage me. I think somehow he knew his words would become an inspiration for me later. They have, emphasizing that I can find my path in life through meditation, and that I have the capacity to live well. It was his present to me, a personal example of his approach to helping others as an expression of the meditative state.

Why is service to others an expression of meditation? How does it benefit us? These are important questions, which can only be fully resolved by meditating. With that noted, I can offer at least a general explanation of meditation as service, an idea with roots in Indian *Karma yoga*.

In real meditation, we experience a condition transcending thought and the self. Again, by "the self" I mean the self that's merely the product of memories and ideas, a self that is born and dies. When we let go of this relative/ephemeral self, we remove the barrier between us and everything else, realizing the distinction between all creations and us is artificial. From spiritual, biological, and ecological viewpoints, we're linked to all of nature or the universe, our genuine/eternal self. In Japan we might say everything shares the same ki; we are all born of ki, exist as ki, and return to ki.

Once we deeply experience our intrinsic unity with the universe, with everything that exists, we feel the life of all living things as our own. For this reason, advanced teachers of meditation embody the spirit of love, which Oki Sensei manifested as serving others. This same spirit prompted Nakamura Sensei to speak out against World War II, indeed war in general, and resulted in his temporary imprisonment by the wartime Japanese government. It manifested in his kindness toward young university students like me, treating us with the same consideration he extended to famous politicians, members of the Imperial Family, and celebrities. The definitive realization of meditative consciousness is always love, a state of interconnection in which helping others is the same as helping ourselves. Extending service to the world causes us to reflect on meditative consciousness, while it simultaneously expresses it. It deepens the meditation experience, and by aiding others we really benefit ourselves.

My short time with Oki Sensei helped me to value this meditation principle. He was reputed to be a severe and strict teacher, and I saw those tendencies myself. However, that night in the dim light of his room, he seemed very kind and gentle to me. His eyes were shining, reflecting the light, and he looked more like a gentle artist than someone said to be an occasionally harsh teacher of meditation. At least he was kind to me that night, helping me to discover confidence through meditation principles.

The Direct and Personal Practice of Meditation

In this chapter I've indicated numerous benefits, which I associate with meditation, and I'm not alone in making these associations. That said, in the end each of us must discover if these assertions are true. There is simply no way I can prove their truth to you with words. Only your firsthand experience of meditation will confirm or deny what I've written.

I'm in favor of scientifically evaluating the results of meditation, and scientists and doctors have quantified some of these effects, particularly on a physiological level. Nonetheless, the ultimate value of meditation ties into the real value of our existence, which each of us must grasp personally. Science has thus far not been able to tell us the definitive reason why we exist and where we will end up, but we can find this for ourselves during meditation.

Chapter 5

MY EXPERIENCES
IN MEDITATION

When I was in the first year of my university life, at the age of 18, I studied yoga-style meditation for the first time under Nakamura Tempu Sensei. It was at a primary school auditorium in Osaka. However, I could not grasp the true feeling of meditation. I can't tell you exactly why.

I think it is because I wasn't serious about realizing the benefits of meditation. I had no negative feelings about the subject, and actually I was optimistic. But my health had been suffering, and since I saw my physical condition improved remarkably by other methods that Nakamura Sensei taught me, I suppose I was satisfied with what I'd been practicing thus far.

Now I regret that I didn't study Nakamura Sensei's meditation more earnestly, because I believe if I'd caught the feeling of meditation at that time, my life would have been different, and I might have contributed more to the world. But later, gradually I came to know more of the benefits of meditation, and I practiced his meditation at home and during group meditation sessions seriously. Nakamura Sensei basically taught the two forms of meditation outlined in this book, but the explanations here are my own, and they're geared toward Western readers.

I also tried various other methods of concentration to enter meditation. Regardless, as I now reflect on my past, I realize my concentration when I was young was not intense enough, and I hope my teachings in this book will allow you to learn concentration more easily and rapidly than I did. In fact, I once asked an electrician living near my house to build a buzzer with a device that cut off automatically after it buzzed for 30 to 40 seconds. He used a part taken from an electric washer, which buzzed to signal that your washing was done. I used this buzzer often for sonic meditation, but it still wasn't possible for me to reach a perfect state of concentration and then enter meditation.

Sudden Realization

When I was past 50 years old, I started suffering from lower back pain. I was often forced to rest in bed in agony. It got so bad that I had to take a leave of absence for six months from the university where I was teaching. One day, I was lying in bed listening to a recorded lecture by Nakamura Sensei. He was teaching how to listen to a buzzing sound to realize concentration as a prelude to meditation. The tape was titled *Shin-jin Meigo*, "How to Unite with Nature." While listening to the sound of a buzzer on this tape, suddenly and unexpectedly I experienced *ku*—the infinite and eternal formlessness that gives rise to all activity in the universe. I finally understood meditation. I shouted out loud, "I've got it at last!"

This was not an ordinary feeling. It was not something I experienced on an intellectual level. Rather, it was the realization of what we can ultimately experience in meditation. This is ku: oneness with the ultimate nature of the universe, an infinite and eternal void brimming with ki energy, a void from which everything emerges from and returns to.

I reacted not so much to Nakamura Sensei's preceding explanation of meditation, but to the moment the resonance of the buzzer abruptly ceased. Perhaps his words served to set the stage for my sudden realization, but I experienced the depths of tranquility as my mind shifted from concentration to meditation. I view this satori as a gift from the universe, and I don't personally take credit for it. In fact, I'm not sure I had any real talent for meditation prior to this spiritual realization. Some of Nakamura Sensei's other students experienced satori while in their thirties or forties. I got there a bit later.

Despite this, I had a profound spiritual understanding that probably was primed by my previous years of meditation. It was a deeper level of stillness than I'd ever experienced, a feeling of absolute nothingness, but a state of mind where I could still clearly perceive external stimuli. After that realization, I felt that my mental state was greatly improved. It was a big change, even though people around me didn't notice anything different about me. I stopped worrying about my back pain, and I soon returned to work.

A Lifetime of Meditation

I worked for 46 years as an English teacher, eight years at a high school, 38 years at a university, and I received the title of professor emeritus at 65. I worked until I was 70. I'm retired from the university now, but thanks to the practice of meditation, I'm healthy. I have no diseases associated with being a senior citizen. Unlike many seniors, I take no medicine.

What I wish most now is to let younger people know the positive effects of meditation and how to practice it to keep their health, attain spiritual realization, and lead a happy life. I wish for them, and all of you, the happiness that I'm experiencing daily. I hope you will practice the effective methods of concentration, which lead to meditation, that I've outlined in this book.

Today, far too many people commit suicide or have psychological troubles, while others suffer from varied diseases and are worried about their health and work. Meditation can help these people, and in fact most people can use it to solve their problems.

Since I realized the feeling of entering meditation through concentration, I've never forgotten it. I use the method of watching a black dot and feel the indiscernible sensation of calmness associated with true meditation. When I center my eyes and mind on a candle flame, I contact the identical state. I've found meditation by focusing my attention on the sound of a rin bell and sensed the same consciousness. There is more than one way to experience meditation, but the basic principles don't really change.

Now I like the rin sound most of all. It is handy, I can ring it any time I like, and the sound ceases by itself. I happened to find a Tibetan bell at an Indian handicraft shop in Nagano. It was so beautiful I bought it. It makes a deeper and more mysterious sound than a Japanese rin. As I mentioned earlier, I sometimes use the Tibetan bell for a change of mood in my meditation practice. Again, after a lifetime of meditation, I've found that the exact technique can vary, but the essential principles must remain the same.

Once you grasp the true feeling of meditation, it's not difficult at all; rather it's natural and comfortable. It will be of great help and value in your life.

New Mind, New Body

My eyes never tire however long I read, and I'm an academic, so I read more books than ordinary people. But I have no problems with my eyes despite my age, which I credit to the visually oriented form of meditation I practice. When I was younger I often traveled aboard, and on these trips I sometimes contracted colds leading to pneumonia, and I constantly suffered from jet lag. As I age, I'm actually getting healthier, and when I travel now all of this has ceased.

Yes, I know lots of people think it isn't supposed to work this way for senior citizens, but not only has my mind changed with my sudden realization into the depths of meditation, my body also changed once I got the knack for meditative practice. Now I can sleep well in any bed, on any kind of pillow, in any country. On the rare occasions when I don't sleep well abroad, it no longer bothers me, and I simply don't worry about my sleep. Jet lag likewise has no effect on me these days, largely because I don't worry about it either; I don't try to struggle with it.

In meditation we often hear external sounds, smell things, and experience other sensory impressions. We can really only effectively meditate when we learn to experience these sounds and sensations, and then in the next instant, let them go. This is nonattachment, and if we learn it in meditation, we can use it in life. Lots of things no longer bother me now that I can experience them and let them go. This is the secret to not minding unpleasant things in life, the secret of remaining positive, and the way to stop worrying about whatever comes. Practice meditation, and you can also do this naturally and without effort.

We create countless problems in life by being overly concerned with what we experience, by in a sense, minding things too much. You may have stomach trouble, but if you can't forget about it, if you're constantly complaining and worrying about it, you'll actually make it worse. Your anxieties can increase the production of acid in your stomach leading to greater problems and heartburn. Similarly, if you contract pneumonia, it will take some time to get over it. Constant worry will only make you feel worse. But how can we experience illness without worrying about it?

This too ties into learning nonattachment through meditation. If you do not master concentration-meditation, you cannot stop worrying about these sorts of problems however hard you try. Sometimes worrying too much becomes a serious illness itself, leading to anxiety attacks and depression, both of which can cause other health problems.

Meditation is a way of being united with nature, so if you practice it, nature is gracious enough to improve whatever trouble you may have. *If you forget your worries, they aren't worries any more.* There are countless things in life that you're better off forgetting. And you will be able to forget effectively if you engage in meditative practice. Forgetting is also nonattachment, and nonattachment is how we meditate.

Learning to Forget

When I was recovering from back pain, I began studying New Zealand's history. It's something I've been interested in since I taught Japanese in New Zealand from 1984 to 1985 at a university there. I was very much impressed by the economic egalitarianism among the people, including native Maoris. I wondered why this island country in the South Pacific enjoys such a high degree of equality among its various classes. So, I began to read about New Zealand's history as I lay in bed recovering, and I hit upon some new ideas and theories relating to how and why egalitarianism was planted in the soil of this nation. I wrote about ten essays on this theme and some others, which I compiled into a book titled *British Colonization of New Zealand*. When the book was published, it received good reviews from historians of Great Britain and New Zealand, which naturally was gratifying.

Yet the book came about because of my understanding of meditation. I knew, and this point is of great importance, that *we forget by not trying to forget*. Let me explain....

If I thought, "Don't think about the pain in your back," this would have actually kept my mind focused on my discomfort. It is the same as trying to not think about background noise while you center your mind on the bell's sound during sonic meditation. The more you try to forget it, the more you think about it. Instead, you should notice the distracting sound, then instantly let it go by gently bringing your mind back to the ringing of the bell. You forget, or let go of the distraction, by putting your mind on something else.

It's really simple, but loads of people don't do this well or even understand it.

I, however, learned nonattachment in meditation, and with this insight, I used my New Zealand research like the bell's sound, as a device to help me to not cling to the pain I was experiencing. Better still, as I continued my actual meditation practice, I began to experience spontaneous insights and inspirations that helped me write my book.

Meditation can help anyone in this way, but it can only be understood via personal practice. Learning to forget, to release our attachment to thought itself, this is the essence of meditation.

Chapter 6

RELIGION, SCIENCE, AND PHILOSOPHY

Religions try to make clear the truths of life; something countless people down through the centuries have been interested in and for good reason. However, many religious movements have based their teachings on creation stories and accounts of ancient supernatural events that not everyone is prepared to believe in without substantive proof. It seems that as the 20th and 21st centuries march on, it is getting harder and harder for young intellectuals to have faith in some forms of organized religion, and church attendance is down in several nations. However, the forms of meditation outlined in this book are not based on such religions, but rather the truest teachings of yoga. Genuine yogic meditation does not require people to give credence to unsubstantiated accounts. This fact is just one way that yoga differs from certain religions. Simply put, real yoga is not a religion, but a meditative form of philosophy or spirituality.

It's difficult for at least some members of younger generations to accept certain religions of the world because of the way of worshipping mentioned above. Worship and faith are, however, not required for the meditation outlined in this book, making it compatible with most religions. I should also point out that the scriptures and sacred books of the major religions convey many truths that are beneficial for humanity to understand.

Finding Our Own Spiritual Consciousness

The general theme in my books and seminars is joining together to study meditation as a basic method for realizing calmness and clarity of mind. This, in turn, leads to the capacity to think for ourselves, and we can decide what is true for us as we learn about the world's major beliefs. It is possible for each of us to build up our own philosophy by doing so.

True, certain people do regard yoga as a kind of religion. But I feel it is not, because there is nothing in real yoga that people are required to believe in. In addition, it is my opinion that originally yoga did not offer any gods for people to worship. Thus, believers in most religions find it safe, and not contradictory to their beliefs, to study the yogic forms of meditation that I teach, as yoga does not interrupt their belief in their religion.

Sahota Tsuruji Sensei, author of books on meditation and philosophy, often indicated that for some people the giant trees of religion appear to have withered and almost died, because of the devastating storm of scientific thoughts. It is true certain people now believe science is almighty and do not find meaning in religion and philosophy. Some individuals do not even think about the human mind. They insist that since they cannot see the mind, it is not scientific to reflect upon it.

The Mind and the Brain

There are numerous people who believe the mind is in the operating system of the brain. Yes, we must admit that we can't have normal feeling or thinking without the brain. But we must also remember that mental attitude affects the functioning of the brain.

If we think with a gloomy mind, the functioning of the brain becomes worse. If we think with a positive mind, it becomes better in the sense of heightened concentration and calmness. We know this from our daily experiences. The mind is predominant over the brain. The mind is more than the brain. The mind is consciousness; the brain is an organ. In short, the mind is not limited to the brain, and science still has yet to reach a definite conclusion as to what the mind is.

If we study psychology, we learn about the subconscious. A number of psychologists insist the subconscious is bottomless, immensely huge. The mind works not merely on the conscious level, but on a much larger subconscious level as well. We can conclude the mind is much bigger than many people think. We just do not notice the vast subconscious aspect of it.

The Limits of Scientific Thought

On the other hand, some people have come to realize that there is a limited realm in which science works, and this is largely the observable and material aspect of life. Yet, not everything that matters much to humanity is physically tangible. We still wonder about the nature of the self, the reason for our birth, the value of our existence, and other significant, yet not material parts of life. Some of us fail to realize that there are parts of life that science really does not address. They may be labeled intangible, but they are anything but for quite a few people around the world.

I'm the first to admit that we enjoy our civilized and convenient life thanks to the development of scientific research, and needless to say, science is an indispensable part of modern life. But we cannot live well on a spiritual level with only scientific knowledge. When we ponder over life and its meaning, we need a spiritual and meditative way of relating to the world.

We live in a world where some people believe science to be a cure-all, but large numbers suffer from neurotic diseases, mental illness, and constant uneasiness. But with the predominance of science, a number of people no longer feel comfortable seeking out answers in religion, leaving them nowhere to turn for help in dealing with a devastated mentality.

A great number of people in our time have unexplainable anxiety and health problems, even though they are materially affluent and well educated by universities oriented toward scientific thought. We have no shortage of intellectual information and stimulation, but still we suffer. In this situation, each of us needs to find our own philosophy, spirituality, or way of thinking about life, and meditation can help us in this direction. It offers something not found in science, and it does not require unquestioning belief like some religious systems. In fact, it promotes a clarity of mind that allows us to draw from good ideas in more than one religion or philosophy, all of which can help us to solve quite a few of the mental and emotional problems that plague modern society.

Science vs. Religion

Quite a few intellectuals today are non-religious, and some have outright antipathy toward a religious way of thinking. Such people regard religions as relics or things of the past, and they sometimes refer to religion as something akin to a drug. Maybe their line of thought is dominant today in certain intellectual circles, but life problems cannot necessarily be solved by majority decision. Majorities are not always correct.

Humanity is at a crisis point in modern industrialized society. People have swerved away from their real selves and feel alienated. They are lost in space like a jet that has lost its controls. Pollution, nuclear threats, disease, and crime all cause social unrest. Why do people today suffer so much? Is there something wrong with modern civilization? Yes, there is. We do not know how to control ourselves, we cannot keep a positive mental attitude, and we lack the ability to answer spiritual questions. And meditation addresses these issues.

How Did We Get Here?

Why has religion lost its influence over certain segments of society? There must be some reasons. If we look at European history, we can see the long process of conflict between religion and science. It is one of the most remarkable reasons religious belief is down within parts of society.

Christianity has a history of persecuting scientists in Europe. Many scientists were burnt to death as witches. The oppression by the church of science, from the medieval age to the middle of the 19th century, was tragic, which is not to say that times have not changed or to imply that people have not been helped by Christian and other religious organizations and charities.

However, about one century ago, science became more powerful, successfully competing with religion in influence even now. This history of struggle has produced a deep-rooted feeling among us that science and religion are two antagonistic fields of human activity. It is as if we are being asked to choose between religion and science. Which way do we go? This is the wrong question, and by the end of this chapter you'll understand why.

What about philosophy? For some, philosophy appears to be an alternative for religion. It has also tried to answer questions about the meaning of life. And philosophy has also sometimes criticized particular scientific attitudes as they pertain to answering inquiries about life. Why did this happen?

While science and philosophy have some common points, they still belong to different fields of human activity and their objectives are also at times different. Science works externally with the five senses, and it studies what these five senses tell us. Philosophy works internally, beyond the five senses, and it considers what the senses tell us and what is beyond such senses.

For example, when we think about the meaning of life, it will be the object of philosophy, because we cannot think about this question using only our five senses. The question for what we should live for is a philosophical one, and science cannot solve it. On the other hand, when we study what materials compose the human body, we can work with scientific methods, because the question can be solved within five senses.

Resolving Conflict with Meditation

The domains or fields where science and philosophy works are different, so it is stupid to regard them as rivals. It is wrong to criticize science from the viewpoint of philosophy and vice versa. It is mistaken to attack philosophical ideas from the position of a scientist.

These days we often observe scientists and philosophers criticizing each other's methodology, but this is not productive. That kind of fighting is like a bird and a fish condemning each other's way of catching food.

Science and philosophy are not rivals; rather they should be good friends, because we can work with both of them depending on what kind of question we are facing. And both of them are indispensable to our living well and intelligently. One can, regardless of profession, use scientific methods and philosophical ways to solve questions in the two different fields of human activity: tangible and intangible, spiritual and material. A scientist should sometimes think about philosophical propositions with a philosophical attitude, while a philosopher ought to consider scientific inquiry and use scientific methods when appropriate.

We can say almost the same thing about the relationship between religion and science. Religion and science can co-exist, if both are genuine. A truly religious person need not exclude what is true in science. Historically, some religious leaders persecuted scientists not due to the inherent tenants of their religious faith, but out of a desire to maintain power and control over society. It was not rooted in true religious belief, but rather a desire for authority and political power. This has nothing to do with genuine religion, and it need not continue today.

What is religion? The essence of religion is a way to admire God or the Absolute and try to be united with it. But as a religion grows to form a large institution (or organized group), it builds up fixed doctrines, ceremonies, and a power system. The struggle between science and religion broke out because an institution regarded the rise of scientific ideas as its enemy. The institution is not necessarily the religion.

Religion and science, philosophy and science can be compatible, or rather we have to make the three compatible. We have to have enough calmness and lucidity of mind to think in any of the three ways according to the situation and the questions that arise at that time. Again, meditation can help with this.

The dividing lines between science, religion, and philosophy are not clear-cut and overlap at times. For example, both science and philosophy may work in realms where our five senses operate. Religion and philosophy function in the same place when questions emerge that relate to subjects beyond such senses.

People who have deeply studied yoga understand well what I have just written, as yoga deals with all the fields where science, religion, and philosophy work.

(By yoga, I mean the essential nature of the word, which implies "union" in Sanskrit. Several forms of yoga exist in India, and only one—*Hatha yoga*—has a heavily physical component. This form, however, is currently very popular and has been often Westernized to become little more than physical exercise. Originally all the forms of yoga—Hatha, Raja, Karma, and others—were profoundly spiritual, placing an emphasis on meditation in varying forms. When I use the word "yoga," I am referring to meditative methods leading to oneness with the universe.)

Yoga is science, religion, and philosophy at the same time, and yoga is not just science, nor just religion nor just philosophy. A true yoga practitioner, who meditates properly, can unify in his or her own self all the three areas of human activity I have discussed so far. Great Japanese yoga practitioners such as Nakamura Sensei, Tamaki Sensei, and Sahota Sensei, as I saw them, studied science, religion, and philosophy. They were able to unite all of them in their worldview, without any sort of conflict. We can do the same.

Seeing the Innate Harmony in Life

Meditation leads to union—yoga—on every level of human existence. It is a unification of mind and body, of the individual and the universe, and it helps us to see the inherent harmony behind every aspect of life. With this meditative mindset, we can unite and freely use science, religion, and philosophy in our lives.

It makes sense to use scientific principles in aspects of life that are observable and measurable. And you have to think philosophically about your life problems, even if you are not a professional philosopher. Rather, you cannot help but philosophize the meaning of your life. This philosophical attitude cannot exclude something religious or religious truths, because both philosophy and religion teach us that there is a world beyond what our five senses can catch. Both philosophy and religion cover the same domain, and religions present us with some good suggestions for living well.

This is not to say that merely joining a religion will solve our existential questions, health problems, or various questions about what direction to go in life. Each of us is given by the universe an infinite power—ki—with which to build a good life. It is there from birth. But for many this remains a potential power hidden in the bosom of the subconscious mind, as yoga teaches us, and we must learn to unearth this great strength through meditation. Merely donating money to religious institutions will not buy us better health or good fortune. But we can discover these things through meditation.

We've all heard the proverb, "Heaven helps those who help themselves." True, and we should help ourselves by exercising our potential energy, which was bestowed upon us when we were born, if we want to improve our health or become successful. The meditation of yoga is nothing but the method to develop the potential that hides in the depths of our mind.

Chapter 7

WHAT'S WRONG WITH US?

There's an arduous problem most of humanity is presently facing. It is mental uneasiness—an unexplainable uneasiness, a bottomless darkness of the mind. It's observed the world over in the form of increased suicides and a growing number of people suffering from neurosis in varying forms. Lots of people interested in meditation are deeply concerned with this subject, and I'm betting you're interested in it as well.

An Irrational Fear

You may have heard of a Japanese novelist named Murakami Haruki. Translations of his books have sold remarkably well in scores of countries because regardless of cultural differences they present topics that people worldwide seem to relate to. The theme in a number of his works is the anxiety and fear modern people are suffering from. Murakami captures effectively how people in this age are crippled by nervousness, unspecified dread, angst, panic attacks, and other harmful psychological states that our ancestors didn't seem to suffer from. Certainly inhabitants of every era have known occasional worry or apprehension, especially if they had trouble finding work or their crops failed, but nowadays ailments like Generalized Anxiety Disorder (GAD) are on the rise, even among folks that are well-off financially, socially, and otherwise.

Where did this uncontrollable and irrational fear come from? Let's start at the beginning...

The modern world produces, supplies, and consumes a huge amount of goods due to the prosperity of industry, technology, and the commercial economy. But this has only been the case for one or two centuries. The industrial and technological revolution is a phenomenon that was essentially nonexistent over the long course of human history, a record spanning thousands of years. For many centuries humankind—whether we resided in the East or the West—lived in small communities, villages, or towns, where we engaged in the primary occupations of farming, fishing, and hunting. It is only toward the end of the 18th century that we see the rise of industrialization in some

European countries. From there it spread all over the world. Before that time, our societies were very different from today, and this was true for many, many years.

Considered from a different angle, old civilizations were group-oriented ones tied together by blood relationships and locality. An individual was tightly bound to members of his or her community by the blood shared with them, and to the place he or she lived. In these traditional settings, the populace doesn't seem to have felt the same degree of uneasiness and loneliness that plagues scores of contemporary cultures. Group labor was the norm in the past because agriculture and fishing—ancient primary industries—required the collaboration of the inhabitants of these villages and small towns. This labor system could be seen in much of the world.

In Europe as well group-oriented social structures existed, where blood relations and place relations tied people together. This was, of course, before large cities developed that attracted workers with special abilities and made individuals with such skills able to live independently of their relatives and in new localities. Group-oriented societies had been a universal community system before this time, and it's common knowledge in sociology that the human community was "blood-related" in its first stage of development, gradually shifting to a "place-related" model. Today most civilizations are "culture-related" ones, if I am allowed to speak roughly. The last social arrangement, a culture-related population, has much to do with urban growth and the rise of market-based economies, which gave birth to the individualistic and less group-oriented configuration we see in much of the present world.

Modern Anxieties for a Modern World

In other words, in the process of developing contemporary societies the unity of individual families and larger family-like social structures has gradually weakened. In such societies, an individual finds it easier to function independently and greater personal freedom is possible, but at the same time many cannot help feeling solitary and uneasy. With the weakening of individual families and a loss of group identity we may feel less "protected" because we no longer live in our hometowns, are cut off from relatives who don't live near us, and live in cities that rarely provide a family-like structure similar to what our ancestors enjoyed in small villages. This sensation of separateness contributes to the unspecified angst plaguing numerous present-day civilizations, but it can be combated with meditation.

Economic change overlaps (or parallels) the social change just mentioned. Living in a global economy where we exchange goods for money has made us feel that the first objective of living is to make as much profit, i.e., cash, as possible. This, in turn, has lead to materialism run amuck, and a lifestyle that's very different from the past when people lived in small villages, where blood relatives cared for each other and numerous members of society grew their own food and made their own clothes. In present urban societies, quite a few people find it difficult to sustain a connection with nature, to reflect upon life, or cultivate an attitude that allows them to learn how to solve life problems philosophically or from a spiritual perspective. And make no mistake—alienation, loneliness, and a feeling of meaninglessness cannot be resolved by a promotion at work or by accumulating more assets. These ills of modern men and women then give rise to conflicts in relationships, indifference toward other people, and an egocentric populace.

Such problems, however, are the tip of the iceberg. Taken as a whole, the varied confusions that can't be solved by our corporations, universities, and banks comprise a spiritual crisis infecting the social order, and such issues will remain unresolved unless we discover the philosophical attitude or spiritual consciousness just alluded to. Certainly reading books like this one can help, but the key to an attitude shift capable of relieving tension and bringing about spiritual clarity is meditation.

False Happiness and the Promise of Meditation

Does it really make us happy to defeat others? Do we "win" if we rake in more money and become richer than our neighbors? Is it real happiness to live in a bigger house than your friends? People in mansions commit suicide. Rich folks make psychiatrists rich, and some famous Olympic medalists go on to have miserable lives. As do the poor and the seemingly less successful. So happiness—happiness that's not a momentary reaction to pleasure—must not be tied to material wealth, fame, or the lack thereof.

What is true happiness? This is a philosophical problem, or perhaps a spiritual dilemma, and at its deepest level it must be solved by meditation.

However, even without meditation, some of us have already experienced enough of life to know that the process of doing something creative, or just constructing something beautiful in an artistic sense, makes us joyous. It's fulfilling in a way that collecting a paycheck is not, and it harkens back to a simpler time. Yet informal creative endeavors, unless they result in fame and fortune, are often devalued by contemporary culture. And we all suffer because of this.

What about doing something to make other people happy? Will this make us happy, too? What if we consciously develop our creativity to benefit others as much as ourselves? How would we feel if we lived this way fulltime; what sort of happiness would this result in?

Meditation involves residing in the present. It is to let go of past routines and beliefs, which habitually lock us into unfulfilling ways of living. At the same time, we stop anticipating a future based on whatever we (or everyone) assume the future must hold. In the present, we discover who we really are, how we really feel, and what's really going on in the world today. This helps us to look at our lives from a different angle, and then things begin to appear differently. Although we may live in a culture where people believe economic profit is all-important, just by changing our viewpoint we see life, society, our jobs, and our hobbies in a different light, the light of spiritual consciousness. In this glow of meditation, we realize that competing with others doesn't produce lasting happiness, and merely making money does not make our lives worth living. Moreover, meditation gives us the strength to fashion a new, more fulfilling life.

Mass Media

Aside from generalized anxiety brought on by social change, alienation, loneliness, and a sense of futility, the modern world is beset by another problem: the power of mass media. Don't get me wrong; there's nothing inherently bad about the Internet, television, books and newspapers ... unless it starts to control and dominate our lives and worldview.

Unfortunately, that seems to be happening. The mass media is indeed one of the most powerful forces in the new world, and the public seems swayed and commanded by what journalists and celebrities say on television, what they post on the Internet, and what they write in newspapers, magazines, and books. Plus, at least some present-day "journalists" are more concerned with advancing their careers and making their employers more affluent than reporting what's true and important.

We are becoming slaves to the King of Mass Media, and we're responsible for whatever problems this causes in our lives and civilizations. The relationship between the media and us is symbiotic, and the media/public problem is threefold:

- ◆ What the media chooses to feature

- ◆ What we choose to consume

- ◆ And why we blindly follow and value whatever is offered up to us.

Real meditation and deep philosophy have assumed a defensive position due to the dominance of mass media, because the media often caters to whatever it thinks will make money. In terms of television, the audience rating determines each program's value, and that value frequently equates solely to cash. Increasing corporate income is one of the most crucial targets of mass media, with the result being that television tends to produce programs centered on bizarre crimes and useless gossip, rather than featuring topics that have a real and meaningful impact on our lives and psyches. Even worse, this growing trend toward "infotainment" has infected the reporting of the news. In this situation, any articles or programs requiring real thought and serious consideration are often neglected. Certainly topics like philosophy and meditation, which need some endurance and profound contemplation, are irregularly featured as they're thought to be "too serious" to appeal to a large audience. As a result, our world keeps moving further away from considering what we truly need to know to live well, resulting in nervousness and discontent.

People know they can obtain wealth and fame if they become a favorite star of the mass media, thus accounting for the trend of journalists, authors, athletes, politicians, and others seeking celebrity status. This has often encouraged those who are talented to become superficial. Even some religions, which we typically think of as being beyond materialistic concerns, appear to be furiously seeking financial returns using the power of mass media. Spiritual salvation, their original target, is being replaced by the goal of making money. And all of this is the outcome of cultures based around only what can be seen with the eyes, cultures in which materialism is dominant and spirituality is waning.

Don't think groups devoted to meditation are exempt from these troubles. Some people are, consciously or unconsciously, attracted by the power and money an organization possesses. Once they obtain a high-ranking position, they try to dominate the association and its members. Then the aim of the group often switches to just increasing its membership and annual income, which gives some leaders a greater feeling of power. Of course, it also leads to the loss of the group's original ideal. If this is unchecked, the organization degenerates, and I've seen this happen to once noble meditation societies.

Look where all of this has lead us: societies in which inhabitants succumb to stress-related illnesses, where selling drugs to combat unnamed fears and anxiety are multimillion dollar industries, and where we're over-worked, living lives filled with material things, but still without any sense of meaning. We search for meaning in materialism when we can't find anything better. Yet there's no deep value in impermanent objects like currency and cars, and we need only look at many lives to confirm this fact. Trying to cling to what's transient is insane, and this also accounts for much of the insanity in modern life.

I'm not saying there's anything wrong with entertainment. But when we lose sight of the eternal and infinite aspects of life, when we focus exclusively on ephemeral and material things, we end up with the problems we have now. And we're at the root of all of this. Mass media cannot be exclusively blamed, as it can't sell us anything we don't want to buy.

Can we avoid this? Can we realize a different world? Sure we can.

Meditation and Meaning in the 21st Century

We don't have to continue this way, and civilization only changes when we change. Yet many are scared to try something new, even when the old model isn't working. This is like an animal confined in a cage for so long that it's scared to leave even if the door is left open. We fear the unknown even when the known contains nothing but suffering. Yet meditation needn't be scary. Just sit a few minutes daily and see what happens. You may discover a different way of looking at life, a worldview that sees beyond materialism and the impermanent entity we think of as our self.

Still, we're often afraid of frugal living. If we don't have a big bank account, an important job, and lots of toys, we feel insecure. This is an illusion; it won't result in security. The biggest mansion, with the best security system, will not keep out depression. Even billionaires can die at any time. Security isn't found in impermanent objects, but meditation reveals the eternal origin of all creations, including us.

Remember, quite a few great meditation practitioners (in various cultures) lived frugally, even enduring poverty, while they sought the truth. Dogen, a Japanese Zen priest, is famous for choosing to live a simple life in remote mountains, refusing the wealth, high positions, and celebrity which political authorities offered him, hoping to take advantage of his vast influence. This is but one example of a person realizing peace of mind through meditation more than though power and riches. But giving up possessions and ignoring your bank account won't automatically give you calmness. The world has lots of poor people who aren't at peace.

So the issue isn't how much you own, but how you view life. The degree to which you're attached to things determines your suffering, and meditation teaches nonattachment.

Therefore even if we somehow were assured of having health, fortune, and fame, serious life problems would not be solved. There are deeper questions than how to get a nicer looking body, more capital, or celebrity. What is self-realization? How can we be united with other people? Where have we come from? Where are we going after death? Is there posthumous existence? Of perhaps greatest importance, how can we find a way of living that leads to these answers? These are spiritual questions, and we cannot be truly happy and serene if we don't solve them.

Using Meditation as a Guide, Forge Your Own Path

You may be thinking that some great thinkers or philosophers have already answered these questions. Perhaps they did; perhaps they didn't. You'll never personally know unless you see the truth yourself, and these problems are simply too important to trust to the accounts of people you may have never met.

Of course, it can be helpful to read books on meditation or spirituality. That's why I wrote this book. But this is much more important—we must be absolutely convinced of the answers to these kinds of inquiries concerning life or deep down inside we'll still have fear and nonspecific anxiety. We can't just reason all of this out; it's been tried fruitlessly by many. This shift in outlook must be realized through a shift in consciousness, not merely through new ideas. This different awareness can use thought, but it is ultimately beyond thought. It's a feeling we must grasp through firsthand experience and from the bottom of our hearts. It isn't an idea, but a state of mind that's then experienced in the body. Answers given by writers on life problems, however famous, are just signposts, suggestions, or guides.

Each of us must think for ourselves and comprehend these questions, not by depending on others but through realizing meditative consciousness. From ear-liest times, differing methods of meditation have been sought after and studied, not only in India but several parts of the world, with the goal being a successful way to arrive at spiritual consciousness. Meditation is the most effective method to experience genuine calmness and nonattachment, and this leads to the clarity of mind needed to answer existential questions.

As the story goes, Buddha was a young, sheltered, and carefree prince in India when he walked out of his palace to enjoy watching beautiful scenes and people. Instead, he came across a miserable man suffering from illness, an old man hobbled by age, and a woman lying dead by the roadside. He was shocked to see them and began to think about pain and suffering in life: birth, ill-ness, aging, and death. If Buddha had been paralyzed by fear of aging, infirmity, and death, he never would have found a motive for building a true life philosophy. He, rather, leapt into the unfamiliar, where he tried to find a universal method to liberate himself (and eventually all people) from misery. Knowing the anguish of sickness and death was a catalyst for him to search for the truth. At that moment he became a true philosopher, who realized enlightenment through meditation.

This story is really a universal metaphor for spiritual awakening; I'm not espousing Buddhism or any particular religion. All of us at some point first encounter death—perhaps of a pet or a grandparent—and all of us are forever changed. This is universal, but how we react to ubiquitous forms of pain is up to us. We can live in fear or use such experiences as a trigger for spiritual realization. If we're attached to and obsessed with our ill health, unhappiness or troubles, we cannot find a way to live fearlessly and spiritually. However using meditation as a guide, we can realize serenity via nonattachment; then pain can be a motivating force to discover the value of our existence and the art of living well. We confront existential questions when we begin to think of the significance of the whole of life.

What does it mean to be human? Where have we come from and where are we going? These and other abovementioned queries are actually universal questions for contemplation. When we try to answer these questions, we're forced to consider what the real "I" amounts to. If our genuine self remains submerged, we function haphazardly, often blindly, and without confidence. This continues as long as we live unconsciously, concentrating only on the surface of things.

Beyond Anxiety, Beyond the Existential Crisis

A famous American psychoanalyst, Erich Fromm, said in *Zen Buddhism and Psychoanalysis*:

> We must consider the spiritual crisis which Western man is undergoing in this crucial historic epoch … There is an agreement among a number of critical observers as to the existence and the nature of this crisis. It is the crisis which has been described as "malaise," "ennui," "mal du siècle," the deadening of life, the automization of man, his alienation from himself, from his fellowman, from nature …[9]

Human beings have tried to follow rationalism since the 18th century; rationalism has transformed itself into irrationality, even though this may sound strange. Along with this trend has come a greater and greater desire to exert dominance over nature by means of the intellect, forgetting that we're part of nature and thus ultimately at war with ourselves. At the same time, the production and acquisition of things has become for many the supreme object of life.

In the process, humankind has become a "thing," and life is frequently ruled by material possessions and property. At times it seems like our very existence is determined by how much material wealth we have. Humanity in the 21st century is heavily concerned with *the perfection of things* (i.e., technology), even though humanity in the distant past, at least in Greek culture and other societies, believed the aim of life was *the perfection of human beings.*

None of this would be an issue if it worked, but countless people are anxious, depressed, and desperate. They frequently discuss the true meaning of happiness in life but have lost the aim of life. If you ask them what they are living for, they'll be embarrassed and unable to clearly answer. Some might respond that they live for their family, others for making money or enjoying pleasure, but in reality few know what they're living for.

Fromm wrote, "Man is thrown into this world without his volition and taken away from it again without his volition."[10] This is true, but we still have to live this life in some way or another. We may feel we were separated from the eternity of the universe by being born. This sense of severance makes us feel like a speck looking out at an infinite universe, causing us to feel solitary and powerless. How can we either endure this separation or regain our unity with nature?

Fromm indicated that there were two possible ways to resolve the issue of separation:

1. Find the unity, which existed before awareness ever arose, that is, before we were born.

2. Find a way to be fully born, to a point of transcending one's own egocentric involvement, and thus arriving at new oneness with the world.[11]

Fromm invalidated the first approach, because to him it was a kind of regression. I don't agree; it is not regression.

One of the aims of meditation in yoga and Zen is to rediscover the unity with nature we experienced before we were born. It's not regression, rather spiritual advancement or progress, but I suppose Fromm looked at these matters from a psychological perspective more than a spiritual one. In Asian spirituality, non-dualistic awareness is frequently fostered; awareness in which we let go of our attachments to the relative world to sense the absolute universe from which it emerges. In meditation we grasp a non-dualistic state beyond birth and death ... the eternity of the present.

Perhaps not being aware of this, Fromm recommended the second solution. I can accept this, because for me past and present, birth and death are one—so both solutions are valid. Fromm's idea of being fully born and transcending the individual ego is also a target of yoga, Zen, and the meditation covered in this book.

Teachers of yoga and Zen say our real being existed before we were born and continues after we die. They've stated that meditative practice helps us realize this.

I say the same. This spiritual realization is nothing other than satori—awakening—the apprehension of which dissolves anxiety and all feelings of separation, insignificance, and powerlessness that plague contemporary society.

Appendix 1

YOGA, ZEN, AND MEDITATION

The forms of meditation introduced in this book are based on the Japanese yoga taught by the late Nakamura Tempu Sensei, and as the result, I thought readers might be interested in the evolution of yoga, it's connection to Zen, and how all this relates to the meditation I introduced in earlier chapters.

Today yoga is unfortunately regarded as mere physical exercise or methods for health in many parts of the world. But this is because most people are only aware of Westernized versions of Hatha yoga, which is itself only a part of the yogic practices in India. Yoga as a whole is a great Indian philosophy with a practical system to realize true meditation. Hatha yoga is an excellent preparation for concentration-meditation. Raja yoga is the form that focuses more on such meditation. These are not different practices altogether, but two kinds of practice that lead to the state of yoga itself, a state of absolute unity of mind and body, self and the universe.

One Truth, Many Paths

A typical practitioner these days often enters the great yoga system by the gate of Hatha yoga, and if he or she is serious enough eventually begins to explore Raja yoga. In Raja yoga, the practitioner practices concentration methods to arrive at meditation. Thus some yoga ascetics are required to practice somatic exercises to train the body and cultivate strength in preparation for sitting meditative practice. It is a useful curriculum, but I believe from my own experience that we can learn meditation without doing so many physical exercises. Nakamura Sensei studied primarily Raja yoga's meditative methods in India, and he did so from the very beginning of his practice under Kaliapa. Eventually, he practiced a bit of Hatha yoga, but this is not prominent in his system of Shin-shin-toitsu-do. Nonetheless, this methodology allowed him (and others) to attain an elevated perception of life, in other words to realize satori.

As I mentioned before, yoga does not require belief in ancient legends or worship of a specific person or religious idol. Yoga is not a religion. Paul Masson-Oursel, an authority on yoga in France, defined yoga as "a kind of practice for self-realization."[12] This definition is correct and to the point regarding the essence of yoga.

Real yogis do not seek profit in this world and salvation in the next world through the worship of someone or something outside of themselves and the universe. A true yoga practitioner should cultivate his or her own philosophy of life by practicing meditation. You can borrow from any religion for that purpose, but yoga is always independent from any idolatry. We can say the same thing about Zen. There is originally no god or divinity to worship in Zen. (I realize that there is no "official version" of either Zen or yoga. Some versions may indeed involve practices similar to religion, but I think this is not representative of the truest and most original teachings of either.)

The world of yoga is so wide and deep that there are many gates to enter it. One entrance is to find a method in yoga to keep healthy. So, certain people enter yoga by practicing Hatha yoga exercises, and while others come to yoga to seek the truth through meditation, and both approaches are valid. Eventually, both types of practitioners may desire to study its philosophy through the practice of Raja yoga or Karma yoga. True yoga teaches us to develop our own power, capabilities, and potential by training our mind and body. It ensures that each individual has freedom of thought, and these are qualities you should look for if you want to pursue any form of yoga, under any yoga teacher. Think about the points above, and realize that not every studio with a sign reading "yoga" is teaching the real thing.

Universal Yogic Meditation and Unity of Mind and Body

The major religions all contain useful truths; therefore a yogi is free to contemplate them. Likewise, these days many Christians, Buddhists, and other religious folks are studying yoga, Zen, and forms of meditation. This seems natural and appropriate to me (and quite a few others).

Yamashita Hiroshi, professor of religion at Tohoku University in Japan, has pointed out the appealing "universality" of yoga by writing, "Yoga is so useful, in many ways, that nobody can monopolize it. No specific religious group or racial group can keep it to themselves. Yoga is a legacy for all humans, as it is tolerant and broad-minded." He also insists that real yoga is not inconsistent or antagonistic with any religion.[13]

Yoga provides a kind of art for living, and in this sense, it should be useful to followers of all religions or no religion at all. Ultimately, yoga is—in all its varied forms—the art of meditation. Some assert that Zen, having its origins in ancient India, is also related to yoga, and like yoga, it focuses on meditation.

"Yuj," the original word-root of yoga, is a verb meaning "tie" or "unite." Yoga roughly means, "uniting"— "uniting the mind and body." The secondary meaning of yoga is to unite an individual with the absolute, because to unite one's mind and body leads without fail to the unity of the person with the universe.

What is the unification of the mind and body, which both yoga and Zen try to teach us? It means to unify the mind (thinking) and body (behavior). That means when you are doing something your thinking is going with the action without any attachments to other things. When you eat a meal, just eat without thinking of any other thing, without mental wandering. This is the most natural way of living. And if you live naturally, you can develop your potential energy and obtain genuine wisdom in life.

Why is natural living so important now? It is because our way of living is so far away from being natural. Our modern civilization teaches us the importance of knowledge, but we can sometimes over-value it. We are inclined to think of other things than what we are actually doing in our daily lives. We think of this and that when we brush our teeth, when eating breakfast, or when driving a car to the office in the morning.

Over-thinking, and over-valuing the importance of information and intellectuality, is responsible for several of the anti-natural tendencies in our time. We are a part of nature, so we must follow the laws of nature, one of which is unification of mind and body. (At birth, mind and body act as one. It is only later in life that some people tend to lose this original and natural oneness.) If we do not follow or observe the laws of nature, we will be compensated for that—usually in the form of illness and bad fortune.

Clearly it is best to live as naturally as possible. Meditation will make it possible for us to live naturally, because meditation leads to coordination of mind and body. When we are meditating, attachments or obsessions are wiped out, and our mind and body are united. When we meditate, we can empty the mind and useless thoughts disappear. Plus, we will be able to unite thinking and doing. This leads to an undistorted perception of reality, which is an essential element of not only yoga, but of the Zen experience as well.

Here is an explanation of unification of the mind and body by a Zen priest. It details the story of a Zen adept's conversation with a monk:

A monk asked his teacher, "Do you make an effort to get disciplined in the truth?"
"Yes, I do."
"How do you exercise yourself?"
"When I'm hungry, I eat and when I'm tired, I sleep."
"That's what everybody does. Can they be said to be exercising themselves in the same way as you do?"
"No."
"Why not?"
"Because when they eat, they do not eat, but are thinking of various other things, thereby allowing themselves to be disturbed. When they sleep they do not sleep, but dream of a thousand and one things. This is why they are not like myself."[14]

Zen and Yoga

As explained in the above story, the average person, driven by insecurity, greed, or fear, is constantly enmeshed in a world of fantasy, without necessarily being aware of it. Masson-Oursel claims, "Buddha was the first yogi known to the world."[15] He seems to believe Buddha reached spiritual enlightenment by practicing yoga. But some people believe Buddha must have invented a new method of meditation, as he tried to defy any kind of convention in his time. I believe Buddha practiced a form of meditation that is not so different from what we know as yogic meditation. There is no literature or evidence to show Buddha's way of meditating was different from what can be found in yoga, bearing in mind that yoga contains many versions of meditation based on related principles.

Japanese Zen originated from Indian *dhyana*, which in Sanskrit means "meditation." Dhyana was *jhana* in Pali, the language of Buddha. Jhana was introduced to China through Central Asia, and the sound was translated into the Chinese words *zen na*. Zen na was later often abbreviated into Zen.

As mentioned above, I feel that Zen originated from an ancient form of Indian yoga, and in an ultimate sense, Zen meditation is basically similar to what can be found in certain versions of yogic meditation. So to my way of thinking, Zen evolved from an early variety of yogic meditation, but yoga's ways of meditation are not descended from Zen.

At one time, such esoteric methods were passed on from teacher to student in India in a way that was often secretive, or at the very least not widely available to the general public. But in recent years, there has been an explosion of information in every field, which has even spread to yoga, making former secrets more easily accessible, especially in English. Today, a great deal of information on yogic meditation has spread to the public in the form of books and on the Internet. The same can be said about Zen.

Erich Fromm explained that Zen Buddhism is a fusion of the rationalism and abstraction of Indian culture and realism and concreteness (practicality) of China.[16] This makes sense in that Buddhism was born in India, and then it traveled to China, where one form of it became Zen, having absorbed influences from Chinese Taoism. I think since Zen was introduced in Japan, it spread and flourished. Absorbing the arts and cultures of Japan also further modified it. And then the spirit of Zen changed them as well, and we can see the Zen influence in such fields as architecture, paintings, *cha no yu* (tea ceremony), literature, and martial arts.

Zen, Art, and Aesthetics in Japanese Culture

The traditional Japanese sense of beauty represented by the words *wabi* and *sabi* seems to be born from Zen spirituality in Japan. It created new arts like *haiku* and cha no yu, playing a very important role in forming Japanese culture. Wabi is an aesthetic sense (or attitude) that tries to find beauty in what is simple and pure, denying ostentation, worldly power, and money. Sabi is an aesthetic sense that discovers beauty in what is old and frugal. The poet Basho Matsuo created a new genre of poetic literature called haiku, which is heavily based on these two aesthetic attitudes. And tea ceremony inventor Sen Rikyu created a new form of art that also brought to light the aesthetic senses of wabi and sabi. (Interested readers can find additional information about wabi, sabi, and a wide variety of classic Japanese arts in the book *The Japanese Way of the Artist*, which is published by Stone Bridge Press.)

Both artists studied and were also greatly influenced by Zen principles. And they were an inspiration to the Japanese people and affected the growth of new cultures in Japan. The ruling *bushi* class admired them for several centuries. (The bushi were, in essence, the *samurai* class.) As a result, the Zen spirit influenced Japanese martial arts. A number of bushi studied Zen meditation and supported it, because to calm and empty the mind was essential when they confronted their opponent. Emptying the mind makes it possible for us to more clearly see the movement of an opponent in martial arts. The bushi often spoke of the importance of the idea do chu no sei, which means "to move swiftly (and promptly) by keeping the mind clear and calm." This attitude is the secret to defeating the man in front of you in martial arts, and it is an ideal influenced by Zen.

Zen leans less on religious books and ceremonies than other sects of Buddhism, as it has no deity to worship. Zen is rather philosophical, and it was popular among some intellectuals, especially in the 19th century of Japan. It remains popular today in Japan, and I studied it in my younger years.

This appendix represents a brief overview of yoga, Zen, and the relationship between the two. Anjo Daza Ho and Muga Ichi-nen Ho, the two forms of meditation outlined in this book, have been influenced by yoga and Zen, as have I. You can get more information about Indian yoga and Japanese Zen in a wide variety of books, in several languages. However, English language books that detail Nakamura Tempu's Anjo Daza Ho and Muga Ichi-nen Ho are much harder to find, being limited at this time to two works written by H. E. Davey Sensei. These are *Japanese Yoga: The Way of Dynamic Meditation* and *The Teachings of Tempu: Practical Meditation for Daily Life*, both by Michi Publishing. With *The True Paths to Meditation*, a third book about these important forms of meditation is now available to English readers.

Appendix 2

SCIENTIFIC AND MEDICAL STUDIES OF MEDITATION

How does emptying the mind in meditation lead to an uprising of energy in us? When the mind is empty, or clear, mental health is maintained, which is linked with physical welfare. After all, the mind does control the body, as can be seen in cases of psychoso-matic illness. So, we can reasonably conclude that since meditation has a positive influence on the mind, it will give us greater energy (ki) and vitalize our health.

Nevertheless, some people still question how a clear or empty mind relates to our mental health. Let's think about it.

When the mind is not clear, it is bound by vari-ous needless thoughts or attachments, often relating to things we are worried about. Such thought patterns obviously lead to tension, and when combined with tension, neurosis can arise, which is undoubtedly a condition of unhealthiness. A clear, empty, unworried mind is the opposite of neurosis and is related to mental health. Neurosis is medically defined as the state when the mind has abnormally strong tension or anxiety, while the state of meditation makes us mentally relaxed, peaceful, and calm. Tension is released.

In this appendix, I'll introduce the important results of objective research conducted in recent years by medical doctors on the relationship between meditative practice and changes in brain wave activity. First, I want to present the results of research experiments made by a Tokyo University professor of psychiatry, Dr. Hirai Tomio.

Meditation and Brain Wave Activity in Zen Meditation

Dr. Hirai was the president of the Japan Psychiatry Society. His research has become well known in several parts of the world, but not every reader is familiar with it, which is why I have included this appendix. He especially studied the relationship between Zen meditation and brain waves. He wrote an enlightening book titled *Zazen no Kagaku* ("Scientific Studies of

Zen Meditation") for general readers. In a moment, I'll describe the outline of *Zazen no Kagaku*, while adding my own explanations that relate to what I've described in earlier sections of *The True Paths to Meditation*. (Readers of *The True Paths to Meditation* should by now realize that the forms of meditation outlined in this book have certain similarities to Zen, and the Zen-related scientific studies and information in this appendix may well apply to Anjo Daza Ho and Muga Ichi-nen Ho meditations.)

First, we have to know what brain waves are. The brain is an electrochemical organ, using electromagnetic energy to function, and the electrical activity emanating from the brain is displayed in the form of brain waves. They range from the high amplitude, low frequency delta to the low amplitude, high frequency beta. Men, women, and children of all ages experience similarly characteristic brainwaves. They are consistent across cultures and country boundaries. The sidebar on page 160 and its accompanying explanations, should make brain wave activity more understandable.

Brain waves appear as electrical changes in the activities of nerve fibers and cells in the brain. So, brain waves express changes in the consciousness of a human being. When the average person acts under ordinary conditions, his or her brain waves are often

A Definition of Brain Wave Activity

Beta	Alert
Alpha	Relaxed
Theta	Drowsy
Delta	Sleep
Delta	Deep sleep

BETA: 12–30 cycles per second. Beta brain waves relate to waking consciousness, outgoingness, logical thought patterns, and conversation. A debater would be in "high beta." A public speaker, teacher, or talk show host would be in beta when engaged in their work.

ALPHA: 8–12 cycles per second. Alpha waves relate to calmness, non-arousal, meditation, and hypnosis.

THETA: 4–7 cycles per second. Theta waves relate to daydreaming, dreaming, inventiveness, and meditation. Suppose a person is driving on a freeway, and he discovers he can't recall the last five miles he's driven. That person is frequently in a theta state brought on by continuous driving. This can occur during other commonplace activities when they become automatic.

DELTA: Up to 4 cycles per second. Delta waves relate to deep dreamless sleep.

beta waves, but a skilled meditator's brain exhibits relaxed alpha waves during meditation, according to a number of scientific studies that can be readily found online. (A contemporary study of brain wave activity in meditation can be found at the website *ScienceDaily*: http://www.sciencedaily.com/releases/2010/03/100319210631.htm)

But this isn't as simple as just sitting with one's eyes closed. Most people's brains do not display profound alpha wave activity even after sitting calmly, with closed eyes, for some time. (And a number of adept meditators, especially in some versions of Zen, usually keep their eyes half open during meditation. What's more, several experienced Zen priests gave off theta waves, which show deep calmness of mind, during Dr. Hirai's studies of meditation and brain activity.)

The Hirai Experiments

According to Professor Hirai's experimental measurements, several distinguished Zen priests initially showed alpha brain wave measurements wider in amplitude, with gradual reduction in frequency. In short, they displayed profound alpha brain wave activity demonstrating a strong level of calmness. Later, they emanated theta waves, indicating a mind that is even more deeply calm and peaceful. Dr. Hirai's subjects were mostly Zen monks and priests from the Sojiji Temple in Yokohama, Japan. The temple represents the Soto sect of Zen Buddhism. One of the well-known and famous priests of this temple was Ishikawa Sodo, who studied the meditation outlined in this book with Nakamura Tempu Sensei, my primary teacher. (This type of "cross-training" was unusual, and it shows the high regard this renowned Zen master had for Anjo Daza Ho and Muga Ichi-nen Ho meditations.)

As I mentioned earlier, meditation gives people deep rest. So, Professor Hirai carried out an experiment to compare brain waves during sleep and those during meditation. The result was that he found that meditators maintain alertness during meditation, whereas sleepers do not during sleep. And both sleep and meditation were found to provide rest, relaxation, and revitalization for those involved.

During his experiment in "mental electrical waves phenomenon," his subjects were exposed to a clicking sound at varying intervals. He wanted to see if they would display "accustoming," and eventually tune it out. When meditators heard a click, again and again, they showed no "accustoming" and displayed alert momentary responses each time, even after they heard the sound many times during meditation. Sleepers were soon accustomed to the sound, and they gradually did not show any response. This experiment indicated that sleepers lose their alertness during sleeping, while meditators do not.

This fact revealed a remarkable difference between meditative practice and sleeping, even though it did not prove that meditation gives deeper rest than sleep. In the experiment, the meditator emitted beta waves for a second or two when he heard a click sound, but then he again emitted peaceful alpha waves after a brief time, and it was repeated again and again. No change was observed. This scientifically proved the meditators were alert and their consciousness was always clear enough to respond to the outer world. It also showed that the subjects of the study were not attached to what their senses reported, allowing them to immediately return to the muga munen state of calmness. They were not irritated or disturbed by the periodic clicking.

Of equal importance, Dr. Hirai also reported that during meditation the activities in the cerebral cortex of his Zen monks lessened, while their autonomic nerves became more active. There are different lobes in the cerebral cortex, which are responsible for different activities:

- The parietal lobe: This is involved in the reception and handling of sensory information such as pain, tactile sensation, and visual perception. It is also connected to spatial orientation, speech, thought, and information processing.

* The frontal lobe: This relates to decision making, problem solving, and planning. It is also connected to reasoning and judgment.

* The occipital lobe: This is involved with vision and color identification.

* The temporal lobe: This has a connection to recollection, sentiment, hearing, and language.

The cerebral cortex and its actions, in short, are tied to cognitive function. The autonomic nervous system, on the other hand, is not tied to waking consciousness and thought. It usually operates below the level of ordinary consciousness, and Dr. Hirai indicated that it became more energetic among the subjects of his meditation experiments. So, when cerebral cortex activity lessens, it could imply a lessening in the movement of thought and the actions of the conscious mind. The same can be said for increased autonomic nerve activity. I believe that this could indicate that during meditation the functioning of the subconscious comes to the forefront, making it more accessible to us. In the depths of our subconscious, according to Nakamura

Sensei, there is something universal for all humankind, something that provides us with access to wisdom and potential energy. Dr. Hirai's experiments just might relate to Nakamura Sensei's idea that during meditation wisdom and great energy, usually hiding in the subconscious, arise.

Dr. Hirai practiced and studied meditation himself and came to reach a deep understanding of it. He indicated in *Zazen no Kagaku* that the most important part of Zen meditation is to just do it. That means only intellectually, or ideologically, thinking about Zen (or any version of meditation) cannot lead us to anything. I agree.

Scientifically Validating the Benefits of Meditation

According to Dr. Hirai, a doctor of psychiatry, outstanding Zen priests in his study displayed alpha waves for a long time, even after meditation, indicating continuing benefits in terms of relaxation and calmness. The word "meditation" is often associated with a religious practice, but by now you should realize that it does not need to be tied to any religion. With the advances in science, and with continuing meditation studies by scientists, numerous people now realize that meditation represents a method to maintain mind-body health. Scientific studies of it have been advancing and increasing; many such studies show it is good for our health in multiple ways. Positive research reports that meditation can have a beneficial effect on diseases like high blood pressure and other ailments, but a detailed accounting of all such experiments is beyond the scope of this book. You can easily find the research, however, with a quick Internet search. Be sure to look for well-established and reputable sources.

When we carry out meditative practice, our consciousness becomes clear and peaceful, which promotes mental health first and eventually physical health. Meditation revives our life energy and power (ki), and I believe it gives us a deeper rest than sleep. Some adult diseases, in addition, appear to be brought about or worsened by one's inability to effectively deal with stress. It is my belief that meditation is useful in eliminating them. Recent studies seem to support this assertion.

Meditation is said by some to have begun about 4000 years ago in India, but scientific studies of meditation began more recently. In 1924, a German psychiatrist Hans Berger reported that brains emit electrical vibrations and that they could show the changes of human mental activities if they could be amplified and recorded.[17] And then scientific studies followed the report, but they were difficult to do because the electricity, which is sent forth from brains, is a feeble microvolt or one-millionth of a volt. But after the computer was introduced into the field of medical research, it became easier to amplify and record brain waves. The study of brain waves advanced remarkably. Professor Hirai used these advances in his important research.

You can read more about Dr. Hirai's studies and theories in his books, which are numerous and well-regarded in Japan. His works have also been presented in English:

- *Zen Meditation and Psychotherapy* (Japan Publications, 1989)

- *Zen Meditation Therapy* (Japan Publications, 1975)

- *Psychophysiology of Zen* (Igaku Shoin, 1974)

- *Zen and the Mind: Scientific Approach to Zen Practice* (Japan Publications, 1978)

You can get a more detailed account of the experiments I've summarized in this appendix in the author's own books. These titles are out of print, but they can still be found for sale online.

Internet searches reveal that studies of meditation have been conducted at Tokyo University, the

University of California Los Angeles, Duke University, the University of Wisconsin Madison, University of California Berkeley, and other major educational institutions in various nations. Most studies have shown that the state of consciousness during meditation is a special one, different from sleep and from that when we are awake. Nonetheless, this does not mean meditation creates an unnatural state of consciousness. There are a variety of times that people, from all different walks of life and engaging in varied activities, display enhanced alpha waves similar to meditation. But meditation allows us to develop this capacity directly and in an organized manner.

Additional Scientific Studies of Meditation

If you have an interest in meditation, the workings of the brain, and human physiology, I'd encourage you to do some online research, being careful to look for trustworthy sources and websites. You'll find no shortage of recent medical research reports on the relationship between the brain and meditation.

In a 2012 *ScienceDaily* article titled, "Evidence Builds That Meditation Strengthens the Brain," a new study shows that long-term meditators have a larger amount of gyrification, or folding of the brain cortex, which may permit quicker handling of information than people who don't meditate. Eileen Luders, an Assistant Professor at University of California Los Angeles Laboratory of Neuro Imaging (USA), conducted the experiments. Luders' work had previously indicated that the amount of gyrification, or thickening, is related to bolstering the link between brain cells and could be connected to the number of years subjects had meditated. That meditation can be shown to physically alter the brain illustrates both the potential of meditation and the neuroplasticity of the brain.[18]

In 2002, the BBC reported that Dr. Andrew Newberg, a radiologist at the University of Pennsylvania (USA) studied the meditation of Tibetan Buddhist monks. When the monks realized a transcendent highpoint, a radioactive tracer was released that let the team observe active sections of the brain. In other words, the scientists observed how the dye traveled to working parts of the brain. Scans revealed a significant increase in the front section of the brain connected to heightened focus or concentration during tasks, along with a noteworthy reduction in the back portion of the brain associated with a reduced sense of orientation and spatial awareness. Dr. Newberg explained that during meditation individuals report a loss of the sense of self and often feel a sense of no space and time. He indicated that this was what was displayed by the subjects in his study, and that he believed that we are poised at a remarkable moment in our history, which allows us to investigate meditation in a way that was not previously possible.

"When someone has a mystical experience, they perceive that sense of reality to be far greater and far clearer than our usual everyday sense of reality," Dr. Newberg said. He added: "Since the sense of spiritual reality is more powerful and clear, perhaps that sense of reality is more accurate than our scientific everyday sense of reality."[19]

In an article in 2012 titled "The Monk and the Gunshot," Tom Bartlett reported on an experiment performed by Dr. Paul Ekman of the University of California San Francisco Medical Center (USA), which showed a significantly reduced "startle response" during meditation. Dr. Ekman tested the Buddhist monk Matthieu Ricard by producing a noise equivalent to a very loud gunshot during his meditation. Ricard, who has been a monk for 40 years, also has a doctorate in cell genetics.

The basis for the experiment came from the notion that involuntary reactions, such as reactions to loud noises, are a deeply primitive response that is extremely difficult to control or suppress. Dr. Ekman and other researchers tested Ricard to see to what degree being in meditation would alter his startle response. Ricard was placed in a room and asked to meditate. A sudden 115-decibel "burst of white noise" was produced, which was equivalent to a loud gunshot. The results showed that while Ricard's facial muscles did react to the sound, the "open meditation" technique he used reduced his facial response significantly below control levels and was dramatically less than when he was not meditating. This is just one of numerous interesting findings that seem to corroborate the idea that meditation heightens calmness and self-control.[20]

Finally, let's look at the research of Dr. David Creswell and Dr. Matthew Lieberman of UCLA. Their brain scans of test subjects showed that those who discharged negative emotions by naming and releasing them through a type of meditation demonstrated strong activity in the right ventrolateral prefrontal cortex, along with a robust degree of calmness in the amygdala region of the brain. The study provides an explanation for how and why "mindfulness meditation" can help to process negative emotions effectively, relieve stress, and improve health.[21]

While these studies, and others, feature various forms of meditation, they all typically involve some form of concentration that leads to calmness, and in this way, they have certain commonalities with Anjo Daza Ho and Muga Ichi-nen Ho. Regardless of meditation technique, quite a few scientific experiments appear to validate the claim of meditators that their practice has genuine and objectively verifiable benefits.

Improving our Lives with Meditation

Despite the fact that doctors and scientists are reporting the benefits of meditation with ever increasing frequency, quite a few folks still fail to take advantage of meditation. Modern people are so busy that they feel it's hard to practice meditation, but if you do the visual or aural methods of concentration for meditation that I've explained, you can meditate at home easily. You don't need to drive to a Zen temple or a yoga *ashram*. In my experience, if you practice meditation, natural healing power will be aroused by it, and healing will become speedy. Recent medical research seems to confirm the positive effect that the mind and meditation can have on the body. But if you fall ill, you should still consult your doctor. I think meditation can help you to recover more quickly, because it deletes needless fear or uneasiness that often comes with illness, and this has a helpful psychosomatic impact on your health.

As I mentioned, I once suffered from back pain. I'm not sure if meditation directly healed me, but I felt stronger and more able to deal with the discomfort. The problem went away quickly once I practiced meditation more earnestly. When I was at my worst, I was dejected, and a doctor suggested seeing a psychiatrist, as he was afraid I was also suffering from chronic depression. But as I began meditation more earnestly, which I had unwisely left behind for some years, I felt it was unnecessary to see a psychiatrist. I now believe meditation can help with depression and so do quite a few other people.

Since meditation calms the mind and nervous system, as medical research has reported, I believe it makes us more capable of handling the stresses in our daily life. Tranquilizers are also said to stabilize our mental state, but they have a host of side effects. One possible negative effect is that they can take away sexual drive, or vitality, while meditation enhances sex. And it has no side effects. Meditation makes it easier for us to refrain from dependence on smoking and drinking, in that we tend to smoke and drink when we are nervous. It also protects us from overeating and obesity for the same reason; many people eat when nervous, and meditation can eliminate nervousness. Moreover, numerous athletes are now also practicing meditation, as they find it effective in bettering their movement. A calm mind makes for a more relaxed body, which can then move more quickly than when tense.

Dr. Hirai wrote that people who meditate find the world they see becomes different from before. The world begins to look more beautiful, and a feeling of happiness arises, without any reason or motivating factor ... at least in my experience. And in my own early experiences, I found I could see each leaf on a tree in a way that was marvelously clear after meditation. The benefits of meditation are truly vast and deep.

Appendix 3

SOURCES FOR INSTRUCTION AND SUPPLIES

If you'd like to locate people to practice meditation with outside of Japan, or get additional information about Shin-shin-toitsu-do and meditation in English, I recommend contacting my friends at the Sennin Foundation Center for Japanese Cultural Arts in California. You can write or send e-mail to the address below:

The Sennin Foundation Center for Japanese
Cultural Arts
1053 San Pablo Ave.
Albany, CA 94706 USA
Website: www.senninfoundation.com
Facebook:http://www.facebook.com/SenninFoundation
E-mail: hedavey@aol.com

Visitors are welcome, but it's best to schedule an appointment before dropping by. At this time, the Sennin Foundation Center represents the best alternative for people living outside of Japan, who wish to learn more about Nakamura Tempu Sensei's remarkable forms of meditation and health improvement.

Tenpu Juku

The Tenpu Juku is my school for meditation and Japanese yoga training. If you live in Japan, it is possible to study meditation with me through the Tenpu Juku, either in seminars or directly at this institute. (Tenpu is an alternate way of writing Tempu, and *juku* refers to a school or academy.) If you can read Japanese, you can find more information online at this blog/website:

www.tenpujuku.com

For folks fluent in Japanese, you can also learn more about Shin-shin-toitsu-do by reading my books and Nakamura Sensei's writings, which are widely available in Japanese bookstores and online vendors in Japan. They carry information about his teachings and the people devoted to what he created.

International Japanese Yoga Association

The purpose of the IJYA (Kokusai Nihon Yoga Renmei) is to make the practice of Shin-shin-toitsu-do (Shin-shin-toitsu-ho) available to people all over the world regardless of age, gender, or nationality. All members are treated equally and varying styles of Shin-shin-toitsu-do are accepted. The IJYA is a nonprofit organization.

I am the President of the IJYA, and the group's world headquarters is in Kyoto, Japan. The daily affairs of the association are handled by H. E. Davey Sensei, who was appointed by me as the IJYA International Chief Instructor and who handles the day to day running of the IJYA. He has received the highest level of teaching certification from this association.

The IJYA aims to make instruction in Japanese yoga inexpensively available to all interested parties, regardless of their level of experience and regardless of which Shin-shin-toitsu-do group they may (or may not) be currently affiliated with. The goal is a worldwide coalition of friends that are interested in Nakamura Sensei's teachings, who work together to benefit each other and society, without conflict or organizational politics. For additional information about the IJYA, send e-mail to:

hedavey@aol.com

Japanese Yoga: The Way of Dynamic Meditation

H. E. Davey Sensei's *Japanese Yoga* contains information about Shin-shin-toitsu-do stretching, self-healing, and forms of physical training that isn't covered in *The True Paths to Meditation*, which focuses primarily on meditation. It has a large number of excellent illustrations, making the practice of the more physical aspects of mind and body unification easily accessible to beginners and advanced students alike.

The Sennin Foundation Center is offering new, signed copies of *Japanese Yoga*. It makes an excellent technical companion to the book you're reading. To order signed copies of *Japanese Yoga*, contact the Sennin Foundation Center. For non-autographed copies, drop by your local bookstore or buy the book online.

The Teachings of Tempu: Practical Meditation for Daily Life

The Teachings of Tempu, also written by my colleague Mr. Davey, offers the most complete biography of Nakamura Sensei in English to date. It presents instruction in Anjo Daza Ho and Muga Ichi-nen Ho meditations like the book you are reading, but in a way that is unique to the author. The intricate details of Nakamura Sensei's worldview and his Four Basic Principles to Unify Mind and Body are also fully outlined, along with some of his exercises for cultivating coordination of mind and body. Advice on integrating his teachings into daily life is presented, accompanied by some of his breathing exercises and healing methods. In addition, the author went to lengths, working with leading scientists, to show the parallels between Nakamura Sensei's teachings and the most current scientific research, particularly in the fields of medicine and quantum physics. The text also quotes from a number of books by Nakamura Sensei, and it is the first work to translate parts of his writings into English.

The Sennin Foundation Center is offering new, signed copies of *The Teachings of Tempu*. It makes an excellent adjunct to my book. To order signed copies, contact the Sennin Foundation Center. For non-autographed copies, drop by your local bookstore or buy the book online.

Meditation Bells and Buzzers

To practice Anjo Daza Ho you'll want a meditation bell (and/or a Shin-shin-toitsu-do style buzzer). This is the metal Japanese bowl-shaped bell referred to previously. When the edge of the bell is tapped with its accompanying wooden striker a melodious gong-type sound is produced. This bell, which is at times associated with Buddhist ceremonies, can maintain a long resonance. Try to buy a bigger bell, of top-quality metal, that will sustain its tone longer.

However, the buzzer used in Anjo Daza Ho isn't commercially available, and not everyone outside of Japan has easy access to a Japanese "bowl bell." To address this situation the Sennin Foundation Center produced CDs, which feature alternating tones from bell and buzzer. Appropriate silent spaces are included for meditation, and you can order these CDs by contacting the Sennin Foundation Center at the website listed above.

NOTES &
REFERENCES

1. Sahota Tsuruji, *Yoga Konpon Kyoten* (Tokyo: Hirakawa Shuppan, 1973), p. 87.

2. Sahota Tsuruji, *Kaisetsu Yoga Sutra* (Tokyo: Hirakawa Shuppan, 1980), p. 65.

3. Elise Everarda, *A Many Splendorous Path* (Hong Kong: Asian Affection, 2007), p. 120.

4. Stephanie Rosenbloom, "What's the Buzz? Sound Therapy," *New York Times* and *Gaynor Integrative Oncology* (November 24, 2005), http://gaynoroncology.com/services/mind-body-spirit/#the_buzz

5. Tamaki Koshiro, *Dogen* (Tokyo: Shunjusha, 1996), p. 35

6. Ibid, p. 86.

7. Tamaki Koshiro, *Tozai Shiso no Kontei ni Aru Mono* (Tokyo: Kodansha, 2001), p.34.

8. Sahota, *Yoga Konpon Kyoten*, p. 70.

9. Erich Fromm, *Zen Buddhism and Psychoanalysis* (London: Ruskin House, 1960), p.78.

10. Ibid, pp. 86-87.

11. Ibid, p. 87.

12. Paul Masson-Oursel, *Yoga*, tr. Watanabe Shigeki (Tokyo: Hakusuisha, 1995), p. 8.

13. Yamashita Hiroshi, *Yoga no Shiso* (Tokyo: Kodansha, 2009), p. 228.

14. Daisetz T. Suzuki, *Introduction to Zen Buddhism* (Kyoto: Eastern Buddhist Society, 1934), p.86.

15. Masson-Oursel, *Yoga*, p. 15.

16. Fromm, *Zen Buddhism and Psychoanalysis*, p. 77.

17. No author, "Hans Berger," *Wikipedia* (n.d.), http://en.wikipedia.org/wiki/Hans_Berger

18. Mark Wheeler, "Evidence Builds That Meditation Strengthens the Brian," *Science Daily* (March 12, 2012), http://www.sciencedaily.com/releases/2012/03/120314170647.htm (Journal reference: Eileen Luders, Florian Kurth, Emeran A. Mayer, Arthur W. Toga, Katherine L. Narr, Christian Gaser. The Unique Brain Anatomy of Meditation Practitioners: Alterations in Cortical Gyrification. *Frontiers in Human Neuroscience*, 2012; 6 DOI: 10.3389/fnhum.2012.00034)

19. No author, "Meditation Mapped in Monks," *BBC News* (March 1, 2002), http://news.bbc.co.uk/2/hi/science/nature/1847442.stm

20. Tom Bartlett, "The Monk and the Gunshot," *The Chronicle of Higher Education* (August 21, 2012), http://chronicle.com/blogs/percolator/the-monk-and-the-gunshot/30408

21. Melinda Wenner, "Brain Scans Reveal Why Meditation Works," *LiveScience* (June 29, 2007), http://www.livescience.com/7306-brain-scans-reveal-meditation-works.html (Journal reference: http://www.psychosomaticmedicine.org/content/69/6/560.abstract)

The following books were helpful in writing *The True Paths to Meditation*, and I recommend them:

1. H. E. Davey, *Japanese Yoga: The Way of Dynamic Meditation* (Albany: Michi Publishing, 2012)

2. H. E. Davey, *The Teachings of Tempu: Practical Meditation for Daily Life* (Albany: Michi Publishing, 2013)

3. Mircea Eliade, *Yoga: Immortality and Freedom* (New Jersey: Princeton University Press, 2009)

4. Elise Everarda, *A Many Splendorous Path* (Hong Kong: Asian Affection, 2007)

5. Erich Fromm, *Zen Buddhism and Psychoanalysis* (London: Ruskin House, 1960)

6. Hirai Tomio, *Zazen no Kagaku* (Tokyo: Kodansha, 1982)

7. Paul Masson-Oursel, *Yoga*, tr. Watanabe Shigeki (Tokyo: Hakusuisha, 1995)

8. Nakamura Tempu, *Anjo Daza Kosho* (Tokyo: Tempu-Kai, 1965)

9. Nakamura Tempu, *Seidai na Jinsei* (Tokyo: Nihon Keiei Gorika Kyokai, 1990)

10. Oki Masahiro, *Meiso Yoga Nyumon* (Tokyo: Nichibo Shuppansha, 1982)

11. Sahota Tsuruji, *Kaisetsu Yoga Sutra* (Tokyo: Hirakawa Shuppan, 1980)

12. Sahota Tsuruji, *Yoga Konpon Kyoten* (Tokyo: Hirakawa Shuppan, 1973)

13. Daisetz T. Suzuki, *Introduction to Zen Buddhism* (Kyoto: Eastern Buddhist Society, 1934)

14. Tamaki Koshiro, *Dogen* (Tokyo: Shunjusha, 1996)

15. Tamaki Koshiro, *Tozai Shiso no Kontei ni Aru Mono* (Tokyo: Kodansha, 2001)

GLOSSARY

Anjo Daza Ho: Shin-shin-toitsu-do meditation on the declining sound of a bell or buzzer

budo: "the martial Ways"

bushi: a classical Japanese warrior, similar to samurai

cha no yu: "tea ceremony," a.k.a. sado

dharana: concentration in Raja yoga

dhyana: meditation in Raja yoga

Do: "the Way"

dojo: "place of the Way," a training hall utilized in Japanese cultural and meditative arts

fudoshin: "immovable mind," a condition of psychological and physical stability

haiku: a short Japanese poem

Hatha yoga: one of the forms of Indian yoga highlighting stretching via the application of yogic postures along with breathing practices

kane: a meditation bell; a.k.a. rin

Karma yoga: the yoga of action, cultivating awareness of our actions and their aftereffects

ki: "life energy," the absolute essence of the universe

ku: "formlessness," "the void"

mu: "emptiness," "the void," "not," "no"

mudra: a gesture used in yoga and meditation, often involving the hands

muga ichi-nen: "no self, one thought"

Muga Ichi-nen Ho: A visually oriented Shin-shin-toitsu-do meditation involving concentration on an external object

muga munen: "no self, no thoughts"

Raja yoga: one of the forms of Indian yoga stressing meditation

reisei ishiki: "spiritual consciousness"

reiseishin: "spiritual mind," a mind that is one with the universe

rin: a meditation bell; a.k.a. kane

sado: "the Way of tea," tea ceremony , a.k.a. cha no yu

satori: spiritual awakening

seiza: "correct sitting," kneeling with the legs folded beneath the hips, while resting softly on the heels

sensei: "born before," teacher

shin-shin-toitsu: "mind and body unification"

Shin-shin-toitsu-do: "the Way of mind and body unification," a.k.a. Shin-shin-toitsu-ho

Shin-shin-toitsu-ho: "the art or methods of mind and body unification," a.k.a. Shin-shin-toitsu-do

Sorin-in: placing the palms upward in the lap, and forming two linked circles with the fingers, for Shin-shin-toitsu-do meditation

Taoism: indigenous Chinese spiritual path emphasizing oneness with the Way of the universe (Tao)

Toitsu-do: "the Way of unification," a.k.a. Shin-shin-toitsu-do

Trataka: a gazing meditation in Indian yoga that is similar to Muga Ichi-nen Ho

yoga: an art, originating in India, for achieving union with the universe

yogi: a practitioner of Indian yoga

Zen: a type of Japanese Buddhist meditation

ABOUT THE AUTHOR

Sawai Atsuhiro Sensei was born in 1939 in Japan. He met Nakamura Tempu Sensei in the 1950's, eventually becoming one of his closest students and obtaining the highest teaching credential in Shin-shin-toitsu-do, a unique form of Japanese yoga and meditation. Professionally, Sawai Sensei was a full professor of English at Kyoto Sangyo University. He became Professor Emeritus of English in 2004. Since his retirement he has had several top-selling books on Nakamura Sensei's teachings published in Japan. In addition, he is the leader of the Tenpu Juku in Kyoto (www.tenpujuku.com), and he is the President of the Kokusai Nihon Yoga Renmei (International Japanese Yoga Association) that promotes inexpensive instruction in Shin-shin-toitsu-do around the world.

Made in the USA
Monee, IL
08 October 2024